Discover the
WORD

*R*eading the
Bible for All Its Worth

Discover the
WORD
Reading the
Bible for All Its Worth

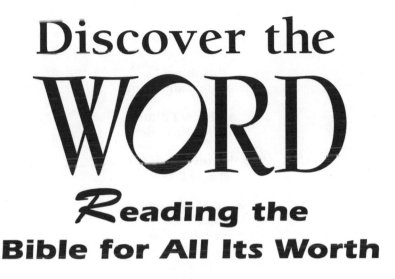

Though this book is designed for group study, it is also intended for personal enjoyment and spiritual growth. A leader's guide is available from your local bookstore or your publisher.

Beacon Hill Press of Kansas City
Kansas City, Missouri

Editor
Everett Leadingham

Assistant Editor
Charlie L. Yourdon

Executive Editor
Randy Cloud

Editorial Committee
Philip Baisley
Randy Cloud
David Felter
David Higle
Everett Leadingham
Thomas Mayse
Larry Morris

Cover design by Mike Walsh
Photo by Westlight

Copyright 1997
Beacon Hill Press of Kansas City
Kansas City, Missouri
ISBN 083-411-7002
Printed in the United States of America

Bible Credits

10 9 8 7 6 5 4

CONTENTS

1

The B-I-B-L-E

by Dan Croy

DO YOU REMEMBER the man-on-the-street interviews? Television and radio reporters randomly stopped people walking down the street and asked them questions. It was a way to find out what the average person thought about a particular subject. Opinion polls are more sophisticated than they were in the '50s and '60s, but news reporters still like to conduct an occasional unscientific interview wherever people gather.

What if a random poll included a question regarding the Bible? What kind of responses would the interviewer hear? Three people—Bob, Linda, and Kay—have shared their opinions with us.

Bob: *I used to read the Bible occasionally but didn't study it regularly. When I felt confused and upset about what was going on in my life, I tended to use the Bible as a good luck charm. I would just let the Bible fall open anywhere and blindly plunk my finger down on a verse. I don't do that anymore. Now I really study the Bible. It speaks to me. I make it through the tough times in life now because of the studying I've done. It means so much to let the Word of God speak to me where I am in my life at that moment.*

Linda: *When I first became a Christian, I wanted to get into the Word of God every day. The problem was some of what I was reading didn't make any sense. There were boring lists of names and places and whole chapters that meant very lit-*

tle to my own life. I'm afraid I got discouraged and quit al-
together. Later in my life, I attended a Bible study where I
learned more about the different parts of the Bible. The Poetry, the Law, and the Epistles all became more accessible to
me. I learned how to dig into the Word for myself and let it
speak to my spirit. I even bought some books that helped me
look up the meaning of the Greek and Hebrew words. The
Word is "active and alive," and it is not a boring routine for
me anymore. I experience a comfort and a joy that helps me.
The Bible is like an old friend to me.

Kay: *The Bible has become to my spirit what food is to my physical body. The inspiration, guidance, wisdom, confirmation,
and joy I get when I spend time in the Scriptures is very
important to me. God's Word has truly been a "light to my
path." At times when I am dealing with issues in my life, a
scripture or a phrase from the Word will come to my mind.
This happens when talking to friends and family as well.
Out of my heart come words expressing care. Before I realize it, I am repeating words and phrases from God's Word. I
believe my time in the Word has reaped benefits in ministry
to others. The Bible has revolutionized my life.*

The Bible?

Why are Bob, Linda, and Kay different from the average person? Why does the thought of reading and studying the Bible excite some and discourage others? How does
one move from curiosity through confusion to comfort and
courage in the Word? The words of the song spell it out:
"The B-I-B-L-E. / Yes, that's the book for me."

The Scriptures are important to our faith. It is through
the convicting power of the Word that we realize our sinfulness and need of God. It is through the confirming power of the Word that we are sustained through life's difficult
times. Throughout history, from the earliest manuscripts
painstakingly copied by hand to widely published 20th-

century paraphrases and translations, the Holy Scriptures still touch the lives of people.

Abraham Lincoln commented on the significance of the Bible with these words: "In regard to this great book, I have but to say, it is the best gift God has given to man. All the good the Savior gave to the world was communicated through this book. But for it we could not know right from wrong. All things most desirable for man's welfare, here and hereafter, are to be found portrayed in it."[1]

Daniel Webster connected scriptural principles with the needs of society: "If we abide by the principles taught in the Bible, our country will go on prospering . . . ; but if we and our posterity neglect its instructions and authority, no man can tell how sudden a catastrophe may overwhelm us and bury our glory in profound obscurity."[2]

Dr. Billy Graham said it plainly. "Our faith is not dependent upon human knowledge and scientific advance, but upon the unmistakable message of the Word of God."[3] John Wesley described the Bible as the source of heavenly wisdom.[4]

In 1974, Evangelicals from around the world gathered to create the Lausanne Covenant. Article 2 of that covenant contains this affirmation:

We affirm the divine inspiration, truthfulness and authority of both Old and New Testament Scriptures in their entirety as the only written Word of God, without error in all that it affirms, and the only infallible rule of faith and practice. We also affirm the power of God's Word to accomplish His purpose of salvation. The message of the Bible is addressed to all mankind. For God's revelation in Christ and in Scripture is unchangeable. Through it the Holy Spirit still speaks today. He illumines the minds of God's people in every culture to preserve its truth freshly through their own eyes and thus discloses to the whole church ever more of the many-colored wisdom of God.[5]

Our three interviewees agree that the Bible is an important and influential book.

Bob: *The Holy Bible has always been more than a collection of writings in our society. My work requires me to travel, and I am amazed at the consistency of the presence of the Bible in the hotel nightstands. It's as if, in spite of the trends in secular society, the Bible is still considered a significant element.*

Linda: *I think it's interesting how people who aren't particularly religious unknowingly quote the Scriptures. I hear people recite a phrase like, "It's more bléssed to give than to receive" (Acts 20:35), and they don't even know they're quoting the Word of God. Portions of the Proverbs show up on greeting cards and in the scripts for television programs. If you ask these same people if they have ever read the Bible, they laugh and say they don't see the sense in it. Isn't that amazing?*

Kay: *I continue to marvel at the power of the Word. I have personally seen suffering people physically receive healing and comfort through simply hearing the Scriptures read. I have seen hardened sinners soften as the Word of God is quoted to them in a gentle voice. Power can be realized in the Scriptures. People who don't know what's in the Bible don't realize the power they're missing in their lives.*

What's in the Bible?

The Bible was written in three languages by many authors over approximately 15 centuries. The Old Testament contains books of law, history, poetry, and prophecy. The New Testament contains the four Gospels (the life, ministry, death, and resurrection of Christ), as well as books of history, prophecy, and the Epistles (letters written to early Christians).

Such a variety of different material can be confusing.

Linda: *I used to feel so intimidated by those who had studied the Bible in seminaries and Bible schools. What I've discovered* *is that those people have not cornered the market on insights and thrilling discoveries from the Word. With a few books and study aids I can find out for myself what the meaning is behind a word or phase in the Scriptures. I may not be able to pronounce the Hebrew word, but I can tell you what it means. The other thrilling part is knowing I can simply read portions of Scripture and not need any study books or research aids. The Word is translated into my language, and it speaks to me where I am. Whether I have to "dig" or not, it still speaks.*

Some are intimidated by the length of the Bible. The famous preacher G. Campbell Morgan once claimed, "The Bible can be read from Genesis 1 to Revelation 22 at pulpit rate in 78 hours." He was challenged by a lawyer who didn't believe him. The attorney was encouraged by Morgan to try this exercise before discounting the claim. The lawyer read the entire Bible in less than 80 hours.[6]

Kay: *My mother used to say, "You can't eat an elephant all at once. You eat it one bite at a time." The same is true of the Bible. When I settle on one book for a few weeks and read a few verses a day, certain phrases and themes begin to appear to me. That's when the Spirit of God ministers to my heart and life. I may not at that time tell you anything about Leviticus, but I can tell you what verse spoke to me today out of 1 John. I want to change my mother's adage to "verse by verse." That's the way I consume the Bible and make it a part of my life—verse by verse.*

The Bible speaks of things in the past as well as things in the future. It dramatically discloses the events of the fall of humanity into sin and God's plan of salvation. It can be understood by the scholar and the uneducated alike. Many young people and those unfamiliar with the Bible do not realize there are exciting passages to be discovered and read.

What a fascinating book! The Bible provides historical accounts of a battle won by retreating (Joshua 8), an axhead floating on water (2 Kings 6), and a donkey that talked to its master (Numbers 22). The Bible recounts the events of the life of Jesus when He turned water into wine (John 2), raised people from the dead (Matthew 9; Luke 7; John 11), commanded weather to change (Matthew 8; Mark 4; Luke 8); and ran profiteers out of the Temple (Matthew 21; Mark 11; Luke 19; John 2).

Bob: *I continue to return to the story of Joseph and find all the drama, intrigue, and eternal issues that touch all of human existence. There is no television program or novel written that can rival the story of Joseph in Genesis. Who hasn't been betrayed, falsely accused, or abandoned in some way? It's all there in the story of Joseph. There have been so many times I've experienced the rough side of life and said to myself, "You meant it for evil, but God meant it for good." If young people are attracted to fast-paced entertainment today, they should read the story of Joseph. It will keep them on the edge of their seats."*

This Powerful Book Changes Lives

The stories are as many as there are believers. A Bible in a hotel nightstand is opened on a whim by a desperate person bent on ending his or her own life. A scripture reference on a greeting card is received by one who feels alone and without hope. A scripture memorized as a young child comes back to one who has tried in vain to run his or her own life. Lives are saved. Hearts are changed. Sins are forgiven. People are encouraged. All this through the powerful Word of God. The Almighty has promised His Word will not return to Him void but will accomplish what He pleases (Isaiah 55:11) and it will discern "the thoughts and intents of the heart" (Hebrews 4:12, KJV).

In so many ways the Bible remains the powerful instrument used by God to communicate to each of us who He is and what His will is for our lives. The Word of God impresses us to echo the prayer the Reformation leader Zwingli prayed before he lectured:

Almighty, eternal, and merciful God, whose Word is a lamp unto our feet and a light unto our path, open and illuminate our minds, that we may purely and perfectly understand thy Word and that our lives may be conformed to what we have rightly understood, that in nothing we may be displeasing to thy majesty, through Jesus Christ our Lord. Amen.[7]

Afraid of the Hard Questions?

What about the apparent contradictions in the Bible, the unanswerable questions it raises?

Bob: *I think I was afraid to really get into the Bible because I thought I would find some contradiction that could not be resolved. Imagine that! I thought I'd find in the Spirit-inspired Scriptures something that would cause me to lose my faith! I'll never forget the time I heard a Bible study leader tell us, "The Bible will never contradict itself as long as you study and read it within the correct context." That has meant a lot to me through these last few years.*

Linda: *I struggled at first with the promises. Jesus said that He would give us whatever we asked for. I remember thinking a couple of million dollars would go a long way in solving some of my problems! Then I studied the scriptures that spoke to the sin of testing God and demanding that He do this or that to prove He still exists. Soon it became clear to me. I don't want to ever get to the place in my life when I'm asking God to do tricks for me just so I can be assured He's still there. He is there, and He cares! When I ask anything according to His will, He is more than willing to do it. It is for His glory that things are done—not to feed my ego or make me feel powerful and in control.*

Kay: *I read commentaries sometimes. I appreciate the people who know so much about the Bible. Even with its tough passages to understand there is still a gold mine of straightforward, simple-to-understand scriptures that speak directly to my human* *condition. Whether I need to grow in my walk with Christ, be encouraged, or be challenged, I know the Word will be faithful to speak to me wherever I am.*

Some experience guilt feelings about failed attempts in the past to be "serious students of the Word." This is an attempt, among many used by the enemy of our souls, to discourage us from being in the Word. *The Screwtape Letters* by C. S. Lewis is a wonderful book of correspondence between a senior demon to a younger novice in the art of fighting the enemy (God and His kingdom). The young demon is assigned a human being who, in the process of the book, becomes a Christian. When that happens the strategies change from how to keep the person from becoming a Christian to making the person think he or she is one and yet live a powerless, secular life while maintaining the appearance of a religious lifestyle. In one letter the senior evildoer counsels the younger demon on how to keep the new Christian from reading the Bible too much. He suggests that the new believer be distracted to read anything but the Bible. A newspaper, magazine, or popular novel will do—*anything* but the Bible. A book that powerful, according to the devil, must be kept from us at all costs.

Are You Ready?

Are you ready to discover or rediscover the Bible? Bob, Linda, and Kay are causing the enemy to run in terror as they pick the Bible up and read, study, meditate, and memorize its precious, life-changing words. Are you willing to discover or rediscover the Bible? There are treasures and promises to be claimed. There are exciting lessons to be learned and applied. God is more than able and willing to use His Word according to the purpose with which it was sent to us. The Word is ready and willing. Pick up the "wonderful words of life" and let them work their wonders in you.

Let's sing it together: "The B-I-B-L-E, yes, that's the

book for me, / I stand alone on the Word of God, the B-I-B-L-E."

Background Scripture: Numbers 22; Joshua 8; 2 Kings 6; Isaiah 55:11; Matthew 9; 21; Mark 4; 11; Luke 7; 8; 19; John 2; 11; Acts 20:35; Hebrews 4:12

Memory Verses: Isaiah 55:10-11

Dr. Dan Croy is a curriculum consultant and a freelance writer, living in Olathe, Kansas.

---

1. Bob Phillips, *Phillips' Book of Great Thoughts and Funny Sayings* (Wheaton, Ill.: Tyndale House Publishers, 1993), 40.

2. Ibid., 40-41.

3. Ibid., 42.

4. Timothy George, "What We Mean When We Say It's True," *Christianity Today,* October 23, 1995, 17.

5. Ibid., 17.

6. Henrietta C. Mears, *What the Bible Is All About* (Ventura, Calif.: Regal Books, 1966), 16.

7. Ibid., 28.

2

What Is the Bible?

by Gene Van Note

THEY WERE CALLED "JESUS PEOPLE." In the lengthening shadows of the Vietnam war, the Jesus People—wearing faded jeans, torn shirts, long hair, and beads—took a muscular form of Christianity to the streets. The Bible became their guide and the Psalms their hymns.

Unfortunately many people could not see beyond their ragged "uniform." These young adults were not the irresponsible, society drop-outs they appeared to be. They were honestly searching for truth beyond what the drug-influenced philosophies of the times offered. They found what they were seeking in the oldest religious movement in the history of the world, the Judeo-Christian tradition.

Often when they parted, they extended a gentle blessing to each other by using these ancient words from Genesis 31:49, "The LORD watch between me and thee, when we are absent one from another" (KJV).

It's a beautiful benediction, but it isn't biblical—at least not the way they used it.

The words come at the conclusion of the confrontation between Jacob and his father-in-law, Laban. In the bleak desert near Mizpah these two men made a treaty. But since they didn't trust each other, they invoked the wrath of God on the one who broke it. In the ancient story, the words, "The LORD watch between me and thee," were a curse, or at the very least expressed a lack of confidence.

The Jesus People were not the first to misinterpret the Bible. Others, with motives far less honorable, misused the Bible long before the Jesus People sang psalms in city parks.

The tragic story of the 17th-century Italian astronomer Galileo is an example of destructive use of official power in a misguided attempt to protect the Bible.

Galileo was the first person to use the telescope to study the skies. With it, he collected enough evidence to support the claim by Copernicus that the earth was not the center of the universe. He first announced his findings in 1609, but his later books caused an uproar in organized Christianity. Protestants discarded his ideas; the Catholic church attacked them—and him. Particularly since Galileo was, among other things, a Catholic priest.

The Jesuits, the order of priests responsible for education in the Catholic Church, maintained that Galileo's published work on astronomy could have worse consequences on the established system of teaching "than Luther and Calvin put together."[1] They feared that his scientific observations of the heavens would destroy people's faith in the God of heaven.

In his old age Galileo was convicted of having "held and taught" the Copernican theory and was ordered to recant. He spent the final eight years of his life under house arrest because he would not discard an idea that has become foundational for all modern astronomical research.

All this in the name of biblical purity!

Like the Jesus People, some folks in their idealism and innocence have looked to the Bible for clever and inspirational sayings. Others, like the medieval church, have used the Bible to support a favored set of ideas. These examples illustrate just two of the ways the Bible has been used incorrectly across the centuries. Neither of them accurately reflects the true nature of the Bible. Our purpose in this chapter will be to move toward an answer of the question, "Just what is the Bible, anyway?"

An Overview of the Holy Bible

Traditionally the Holy Bible has been bound in black leather, inscribed in gold, and printed on linen or high-quality bond paper. Modern translations come in all sizes, shapes, colors, and quality. You can buy them most anywhere, from the grocery store to the corner bookstore.

But the Bible is unlike any other book. Unless it is a reference book, like a dictionary, we expect a book to be written so we can read it from the first page to the last. Good writers put in transitions so the story flows from one chapter to the next, with the conclusion coming in the final chapter or on the last page. Anyone with adequate reading skills should be able to read a book this way and understand what the writer is trying to say.

But not the Bible.

The newcomer to the Bible who tries to read consecutively from Genesis to Revelation is headed for confusion. The Bible is more like a library of 66 books collected under one cover and organized into two sections, the Old Testament and the New Testament.

The Holy Bible was not written by one person nor by a group of people working together. Not even by a collection of people who belonged to the same generation. The sacred book of Christianity, the Holy Bible, is a library assembled over a period of approximately 1,500 years. Forty writers authored its pages, using three languages: Hebrew, Aramaic, and Greek. The writers included both the educated and the untrained: kings, farmers, poets, public officials, doctors, military generals, teachers, and preachers.[2]

Nor is there anything unusual about the word "Bible." Originally, the word referred to the inner bark of the papyrus reed used as the raw material for ancient paper. Then the word identified a collection of papyrus sheets. Finally, it came to mean any bound volume. Simply stated, "a book."

All this raises valid questions. Is the Bible one book or

a collection of essays and short stories? Is the Bible a collection of real events or merely an assortment of the myths of humans? These and similar questions will be dealt with in this chapter and throughout this book. But we need a place to stand as we proceed. Here is a working definition of what the Bible is. Let's use it as a foundation on which to build our understanding of the Bible.

The Bible is the Spirit-inspired, written record revealing one message of who God is and how He wants to relate to men and women in ways that will bring salvation and peace to them.

Historical Importance of the Holy Bible

The Bible has influenced history in surprising and dramatic ways. We will look at three examples to illustrate the place of the Bible in history. Here we use the word "Bible" to refer to both the Old and New Testaments or to either of them standing alone.

Josiah, grandson of Manasseh, became the 16th king of Judah at age 8 when his father, Amon, was murdered in 640 B.C. His grandfather was the most wicked king in Judah's history. His father stood second in that tragic line of spiritual failure.

Fortunately, Josiah fell under the influence of advisers who worshiped the God of David. By the time he was 16, he actively sought the God his father and grandfather rejected. When he was 20, he began to remove pagan worship from Judah. Six years later, he launched a program to cleanse and repair the Temple in Jerusalem. During the repair, a "Book of the Law" was found and later read to Josiah. (See 2 Kings 22, especially verse 8.) Using this holy book as his guide, Josiah led Judah in a time of spiritual renewal—the last great revival in the history of their nation. All because a lost book, the holy Word, was found—a book that had been lost, of all places, in the Temple.

The greatest spiritual reform movement in modern

times was led by Martin Luther. Luther, trained as a Roman Catholic monk in the Augustinian tradition, was a professor of Bible and theology at the University of Wittenburg in Germany. His personal conversion came during his study of Romans and Galatians. Instructed to recant, Luther said, "My conscience is captive to the Word of God . . . Here I stand, I can do no other." When the pope placed him under severe sanction, Luther hid out in the castle of Wartburg. There, from 1520 to 1534, he translated the Hebrew Old Testament and the Greek New Testament into easy-to-read German. "The completed Luther Bible proved to be no less tremendous a force in the German-speaking world than the King James Version was later in the English sphere, and it must be regarded as one of Luther's most valuable contributions."[3]

Preceding Luther was a brave Englishman named John Wycliffe. He has been called the Morning Star of the Reformation. Wycliffe believed the way to prevail against an abusive and entrenched papal bureaucracy was by giving the common people the Bible in their own language. He was so hated by ecclesiastical authorities that, several decades after his death, his body was dug up, burned, and the ashes thrown into the Swift River. Others followed Wycliffe. William Tyndale was another of the scholars who translated the Bible into English. For his efforts he was strangled and burned at the stake.

They, and those who followed them in Bible translation, have made available the most widely printed book in the history of the world. It has been translated into all the major languages, and hundreds and hundreds of minor tongues and dialects.

Why would people give their lives for such a task, many of them knowing their lives would be in danger? Simply because they had been changed by the Bible and wanted to extend that transforming power to everyone who lives on the face of the earth. They understood that the Bible is a book about God, about God and humans, about God revealing himself to humans for the purpose of bringing salvation to the world.

Let's add another piece to the structure we are building. Earlier we said, "The Bible is the written record revealing one message of who God is and how He wants to relate to men and women in ways that will bring salvation and peace to them."

Now we can say all the more simply: **The Bible is "salvation history."**

Let's look more closely to see what that means.

A Close-up Look at the Bible

Adam. The special relationship between God and humans began very early in time. The Bible tells us that God chose to make Adam in His own image (Genesis 1:26). We're informed that the Lord walked with our first ancestors in the garden (3:8). Why did the Lord act this way? We're not told directly. However as the story unfolds, it becomes clear that God chose to create persons with whom He could have a close personal relationship.

Then Adam and Eve, his wife, decided to do something God had expressly forbidden (chap. 3). The Bible calls their choice "sin." Their action fractured the loving relationship God created and set the stage for the drama of the biblical story. For instead of the Lord rejecting them or destroying them, He reached out to them in love. The first promise of salvation comes in verse 15, which, on reflection, Bible scholars in faraway generations see as the first promise that ultimately would be fulfilled when a Baby was born in Bethlehem in the days of Herod the king.

Salvation history had begun.

Noah. As the story progressed in Genesis, no one walked alone; God was always nearby. As the generations passed, Adam and Eve's family grew, not only in numbers but in evil. Finally, God would tolerate no more. He chose one righteous man, Noah, and his family. When they were secure in a specially constructed boat called an ark, the Lord allowed the rain to fall until all were lost but this one family.

When the floods abated and Noah's family left the ark, the Lord placed the rainbow in the sky as a sign of His presence. He said, "This is the sign of the covenant I am making between me and you and every living creature with you, a covenant for all generations to come" (9:12).

Salvation history continued, this time with the family of Noah.

Early on in the Bible a pattern appears. Neither God's love nor His judgment were remembered very long. Repeatedly, in one way or another, the God of creation and companionship was replaced by selfish interests and the gods of human imagination. The tragedy of the Tower of Babel (chap. 11) illustrates this human tendency. But God did not give up.

Abraham. Out of the confusion, heartache, and tragedy of the early days of the human race, the Lord found one man he could trust, Abram—or as he is more commonly known, Abraham (chaps. 12—25). God said to Abraham, "I will establish my covenant as an everlasting covenant between me and you and your descendants after you for the generations to come, to be your God and the God of your descendants after you" (17:7). Known as the Abrahamic covenant, this was one of the watershed moments of the Old Testament.

Salvation history continued.

From Jacob to Moses. The next key person in the story of human redemption was Abraham's grandson, Jacob. The story (chaps. 25—35) needs to be read, for it is too long to be recounted here. Of special interest to us is the fact that Jacob had 12 sons who became the fathers of the 12 tribes of Israel. Soon it became clear that God had chosen the Israelites to be the vehicle by whom He would bring salvation to the world.

Famine drove Jacob's family to Egypt. From there, generations later, they emerged as a nation under the leadership of a man named Moses.

East of Egypt and south of modern Israel, the people of the Exodus stopped at a barren mountain called Sinai. There the God of creation and salvation provided a new set of guidelines for living—among those are the familiar, though often ignored, Ten Commandments and the promise of God's blessing if they would obey His words. The Exodus and Sinai transformed some ragtag slaves into a nation—a covenant people who had no earthly king. The Lord Jehovah was their king.

Salvation history continued.

The Promise to David. As their fortunes increased and they adapted to the land God had given them, the Israelites often took on the ways of the people around them—especially their gods. Ultimately, they wanted a king like their neighbors. Saul was appointed; then replaced by David, the greatest king of all. To David the Lord said, "Your house and your kingdom will endure forever before me; your throne will be established forever" (2 Samuel 7:16).

Christians have interpreted this, and other promises from God to David, as the basis for the expectation that a Savior would come who would bring redemption to His people in a new way. This covenant promise was fulfilled when an angel appeared to a man named Joseph and said, "Do not be afraid to take Mary home as your wife, because what is conceived in her is from the Holy Spirit. She will give birth to a son, and you are to give him the name Jesus, because he will save his people from their sins" (Matthew 1:20-21).

Conclusion

In these brief words we have swept across the pages of the entire Old Testament. Space has forced us to omit far more than we included. Yet, our purpose has been to take a quick look at what the Bible *is*, not an in-depth study of what the Bible *says*. It's vitally important for us to see that the covenant people provide the frame of reference for understanding the meaning of the coming of Jesus Christ as our Savior.

In Christ, salvation history is given a name, a face, a new message, and a new promise. His life, death, and resurrection provide the proof that He is able to keep the promise of the angel to Joseph, "He will save his people from their sins" (Matthew 1:21). The Gospel stories of Matthew, Mark, Luke, and John tell us about Jesus. The history of the Early Church is recounted in the Acts of the Apostles as well as in the letters of Paul and other church leaders. All these describe how the redemption brought by Jesus to the world has crossed all cultural, ethnic, and national boundaries. This is the story of the history of salvation—a story that is still unfolding as the gospel is shared with our generation. Someday there will be an end to the story. The Book of Revelation describes a time when salvation history will be complete, when God through Christ will set up His kingdom forever, and a return to an Eden-like world will be accomplished—a world where God can again proclaim, "And it was good."

And so we conclude with this definition: **The Bible is the Spirit-inspired written revelation of God, who lovingly calls us to respond to His love by faith that leads to salvation and eternal life.**

Background Scripture: Genesis 1:26; 3:8, 15; 9:12; 11—35; 17:7; 2 Samuel 7:16; 2 Kings 22:8; Matthew 1:20-21

Memory Verses: 2 Timothy 3:16-17

Rev. Gene Van Note is the former executive editor of adult Sunday School materials for the Church of the Nazarene. He is retired and lives in Overland Park, Kansas.

---

1. "Galileo," *The New Encyclopedia Britannica* (Chicago: Encyclopedia Britannica, Inc., 1985), 19:641.
2. Throughout this book we refer to 40 authors of the Bible. Scholars have various opinions as to whether the number is actually more or less than 40. We have chosen to use the "traditional" number in this book, while recognizing that this issue is open.
3. J. D. Douglas and Philip W. Comfort, eds., *Who's Who in Christian History* (Wheaton, Ill.: Tyndale House, 1992), 434.

3

Ancient Writers of a Living Story

by Timothy L. Thomas

"FATHER, SEE HOW BRIGHT THE STARS ARE TONIGHT. Please tell the story again," implored young Isaac. Abraham threw a log on the fire and settled back on his mat in front of the tent. Then, gazing into the night sky, he repeated the ancient words: "In the beginning God created the heavens and the earth . . ."

The Bible is a divine-human Book, as Christ is the divine-human Person. This is the key that unlocks the door to an understanding of the true nature of the Scriptures. God could have sent His Son in adult human form without a human birth. Jesus' body would then have been simply a shell encasing the divine nature. However, God in His wisdom did not choose to do it that way. Rather, He caused His Son to be born of a woman. In that way Jesus shared the personality and physical characteristics of His mother. He not only bore resemblance to her in His facial features but also was influenced by the intellectual and social atmosphere of the home.

So it was with the Bible. God could have sent down the Book already inscribed with the complete revelation, bound in black leather, gold-edged, and silk-sewn. He did not choose to do so. Instead, the light of divine revelation broke in on the souls of Moses, David, Paul, John, and many others. The result is a divinely inspired, humanly written revelation of God's truth for us.

Just as sunlight when conducted through a prism is broken down into its various rays, so the light of God's truth when filtered through the prisms of human personalities took on the varying slants and interests of those personalities. That is shown not only in the language used—both vocabulary and style—but also in thought-forms, in ways of approach, in diversity of emphasis. The Holy Spirit used the varying interests and emphases of the different writers to convey the total of divine revelation in the Bible.

It is unfortunate that too often we see only one side of the truth, and so we actually have only a half-truth. If we were to ask the question, "Was Jesus divine or human?" some might emphatically answer, "Divine!" while others might reply, "Human!" Both are right, and both are wrong. Jesus was both human *and* divine.

The same situation holds true in relation to the Scriptures. Some Christians emphasize the *divine* source of the Bible until they sometimes neglect the *human* origin. Other Christians sometimes do just the opposite. The Bible did have a human origin; it came from the hands of men who wrote it. Yet its ultimate source was divine; the Holy Spirit inspired the writers. This gives it its unique authority as the Word of God.

One person sees only the scribe sitting at a desk, pen in hand, writing the words of scripture and declares, "The Bible is a human book." Another sees only the inspiring Spirit hovering overhead and cries, "It is divine!" What we need is to see the whole picture, not just one part of it. The Bible is a divine-human Book.

The Writing of the Book

The earliest portions of Scripture arose from the Spirit-inspired accounts of the wonders of God in individual and community life. These stories were carefully told over and over again around the campfires of the nomadic Israelites. Over time, these stories were eventually written down by people like Moses. Later, as papyrus and parchment became more accessible, written records of history, worship, poetry, prophecies, and much later during the time of the Early Church, purposely crafted accounts of Jesus' life and letters to churches were preserved and eventually incorporated into our Scriptures.

Baruch looked up from his writing as Jeremiah continued to pace up and down. "Is that all, sir?" inquired Baruch. Jeremiah thought a while and then responded, "Yes, all for now. Take the manuscript and read it to the people in the Temple." Baruch waited for the ink to dry and then rolled up the manuscript. Leaving the house, he hurried up the hill to the Temple.

Without word processors or typewriters, the original writing of the Book was laborious. None of the original manuscripts remain, although there are many very old copies that scholars study. Jeremiah 36 gives us the fascinating account of how a part of Scripture was put on paper. From this passage we know that pen and ink were used to write on scrolls. It is clear that all of Scripture had to go through the process of being written down.

The Bible is actually a library of 66 books written over a period of years. The 39 books of the Old Testament took about 1,000 years to appear (roughly 1400-400 B.C.). The 27 books of the New Testament were written in a much shorter span of time, about 50 years (A.D. 45-95). How did these 66 books finally come to be bound in one volume called "the Bible"? How did "the books" become "the Book"?

The word "canon" is used when we talk about the process of the individual 66 books becoming one Book. The word "canon" simply means an officially accepted list of books. The process of collecting and accepting as authoritative the individual books of our present-day Bible took time and thought. Our Old Testament is essentially the same Scriptures the Jews accepted over 2,000 years ago. The Old

Testament took on its final shape about 400 years before Christ. But when Jerusalem was destroyed in A.D. 70, official action was called for to set the exact limits of Scripture. In response, Jewish rabbis officially closed the canon of the Old Testament in A.D. 90 including, though in different order than our Bibles, the same 39 books we recognize today.

About A.D. 140 an influential early Christian (later labeled a heretic) named Marcion adopted as his New Testament 10 Epistles of Paul and only one of the Gospels. He also rejected the entire Old Testament. To counteract this kind of individual selection of Scripture, the Church had to think about fixing the limits of what should be considered as Scripture. Over the following decades, many discussions ensued about what should and should not be viewed as authoritative scripture. The first exact list of our current 27 New Testament books that we have record of is found in a letter written by an early Christian leader in A.D. 367. Finally in A.D. 397 the Church officially decreed that the only "canonical" New Testament books worthy of being read in churches were the 27 books we find in our Bibles today. From that day, the Church has maintained that the canon of Scripture is closed; no new books will be added and no books will be deleted from our Scriptures. We believe the Holy Spirit led to the selections that were made.

Many other books were written during the biblical era, especially during the period immediately preceding the coming of Christ, which also claimed to be the Word of God. Sometimes reference is made to the Apocrypha, a group of books that sound scriptural and are still included in Catholic Bibles. The Protestant Church, however, under the guidance of the Holy Spirit over many years evaluated all of these documents and came to an agreement that the 66 books of the Old and New Testaments would be considered authoritative and complete.

The written Word of God exists as a revealer of the living Word of God, namely Jesus Christ. The whole of Scripture is a testimony to Christ. That is why Christians refer to the "Old" and "New" Testaments—they are testimonies to the person and work of Jesus.

Copying the Book

Committed and careful work was needed to preserve the integrity of the sacred text over many centuries. Before the invention of printing around A.D. 1455, all Scripture was copied by hand—a labor-intensive and expensive process. The Dead Sea Scrolls are an example of some of the very earliest, hand-copied manuscripts of the Bible. Copying a Bible took a long time and was always subject to copying errors. Copying errors could arise from fatigue, poor eyesight, or mispronunciation.

In addition to the mechanics of copying manuscripts, scribes faced the problem that chapter and verse markings were absent in the original texts. Word spacing and punctuation were also nonexistent. For example, New Testament manuscripts were a long series of letters without ways to identify the end of sentences. *ThismadetheBibleverydifficulttoread.* To counteract these problems, scribes invented systems of counting letters to make sure that nothing was left out. Also checking references was a laborious process of unrolling long scrolls and looking for a particular passage.

All in all as we look over the many centuries, it is indeed a miracle of God that His Word has been preserved with great accuracy. While it is to be acknowledged that there are variant readings arising from the various existing documents, very few of these variants make a significant difference and none of them affect Christian doctrine. This level of accuracy is attributable to the supervision of the Spirit of God both in the original writing and also in the special work of copying the manuscripts. It is certainly appropriate to include this copying process as a part of the whole understanding of the inspiration of Scripture. God inspired Scripture when it was originally written and also guided the process as it was copied, translated, and read down through the centuries.

As the centuries passed by, hand-copied versions of Scripture became costly treasures, so the Bible was not readily available to all. Wealthy people and the clergy had primary access to the Bible. The less educated and poorer people had to depend on others for their knowledge of the Bible. Gradually the clergy came to control the availability of the Bible. This limitation probably arose as a practical matter since somebody needed to look after the Bible. However, two problems were soon apparent. First, the copies of the Bible during those early days were available only in Hebrew, Greek, and Latin, which fewer and fewer people read. Second, the clergy became the official interpreters of the Bible.

It soon became clear to many that if the message of the gospel were to flourish, then the Bible had to be made available to all in the common languages of the people. Renewed emphasis on learning during the Renaissance generated efforts in this direction, which in turn often ran into resistance.

Resistance to the Book

Now for a moment, let us go back to Jeremiah for an illustration of resistance to the Word of God.

Baruch, Jeremiah's scribe, took the written Word up to the Temple, where it was read. The message of repentance was received and a time of fasting was proclaimed (Jeremiah 36:9). Sadly, however, the king was not in sympathy with the message. He called for the scroll and had it read to him. Jeremiah tells us:

It was the ninth month and the king was sitting in the winter apartment, with a fire burning in the firepot in front of him. Whenever Jehudi had read three or four columns of the scroll, the king cut them off with a scribe's knife and threw them into the firepot, until the entire scroll was burned in the fire (Jeremiah 36:22-23).

31

The king showed no fear even when his associates told him not to burn the scroll. Instead the king ordered the arrest of Jeremiah and Baruch. However, that was not to be, for "the LORD had hidden them" (v. 26). When Jeremiah received word that the king had burned the scroll, he began dictating again.

Even as prophets were not always popular, so sometimes written messages from God were rejected and efforts were made to stamp them out. Throughout history it seems that often those who could read the Scripture were afraid that if the Bible were made widely available, by making many copies or translating it into the language of the people, they could not control how it would be interpreted. The newer readers might come up with new ideas that would conflict with tradition. However, the real power of Scripture has been its ability to revive the Church just in this way. For example, during the Reformation when the Protestant movement began, people read the Bible for themselves and rediscovered important truths that were then used to reevaluate tradition. Salvation by faith rather than by works was one of these important truths.

Translating the Book

It was God's plan that the Word, written down over many centuries, would be available to all humanity. However, when finished in written form, Scripture was not in every language (such as English). The Old Testament was mostly in Hebrew, with some very small sections in Aramaic, and the New Testament was written in Greek. Obviously, if the Bible were for all people, then it had to be made available in all languages. Since not everyone, even in Jesus' day, read Hebrew and Greek, translations had to be made. At least 100 years before Christ, the Old Testament had been translated into Greek. This Greek text, known as the Septuagint, was the Scripture of the Early Church.

In A.D. 384, Jerome's Latin translation, known as the

Vulgate, replaced the Latin versions of the time and became the standard for centuries. In medieval times, a number of Anglo-Saxon Bibles were produced.

Just as serious debate surrounded the settlement of the final books to be included in Scripture, so too debate surrounded the translation of Scripture. At times the controversy resulted in the execution of those who tried to translate the Bible into the common languages of the times.

In spite of much antagonism, English translations by Tyndale (1525) and Coverdale (1535) were produced. These were followed by the Great Bible (1539), the Geneva Bible (1560), and the Bishop's Bible (1568). As the political and church climate changed, so did the fortunes of Bible translators. All of this activity eventually led to the production of the King James Version of the Bible in 1611. In 1613, 1629, and 1638 significant revisions were made to this Bible. Then in 1769 a final revision was made that especially modernized its spelling. It is this final revision of the King James Version that became the definitive English work for the next 300 years.

As with many new translations of the Bible throughout history, even the King James Version suffered ill feelings at first. A noted Bible scholar of that day expressed the view of many when he said: "[The King James Version] bred in me a sadness that will grieve me while I breathe, it is so ill done. Tell His Majesty that I had rather be rent in pieces with wild horses, than any such translation by my consent should be urged upon poor churches . . . The new edition crosseth me. I require it to be burnt."[1]

Particularly of note in this period is the story of Hugh Latimer. Latimer, who lived in the time of Henry VIII (1500s), was finally burned at the stake for his evangelical position on Scripture and the sacraments. He had spent his life in the educational work of trying to make the Bible available in common English. Finally, as he and his friend Ridley were tied to the stake, Latimer called out: "Be of good comfort, Master Ridley, and play the man. We shall this day light such a candle, by God's grace, in England as I trust shall never be put out."[2]

Centuries have passed, and because of the evangelical spirit and sacrifices of such men as Wycliffe and Latimer, the Bible is commonly available in our own language. The awesome work of proclaiming the truth of the gospel to combat ignorance, confusion, and sin in an increasingly secular age still continues. The translation of the Bible into newer English translations and a wide number of other languages is a major aspect of this work and is being carried on today with devotion.

Yet the Bible is a very ancient book. It has much that, at first look, seems only relevant to a small nation of desert people or to a Mediterranean culture of centuries ago. If God has so miraculously kept His book available in spite of fire and sword and has thereby provided it in our language, there must be a reason. The reason is that this Book contains the only true message of salvation that speaks to all times and cultures. Nevertheless, it must be understood today in such a way that it makes a difference in our daily lives. It must be understood and applied as the living truth, not just kept as a dusty heirloom.

Background Scripture: Jeremiah 36; 2 Peter 1:20-21; John 1

Memory Verses: 2 Peter 1:20-21

Dr. Timothy L. Thomas is associate academic dean and professor of Christian ministries at Asbury College, Wilmore, Kentucky.

Portions of this chapter have been excerpted from Ralph Earle's *How We Got Our Bible* (Kansas City: Beacon Hill Press of Kansas City, 1971).

1. F. F. Bruce, *The English Bible: A History of Translations* (New York: Oxford University Press, 1961), 107.

2. C. H. Stuart, ed. *Latimer,* vol. 1 of *Oxford History of England Series* (New York: Oxford University Press, 1962), 339.

4

Bridging the Culture Gap

by Randy Cloud

MANY OF US HAVE HAD THE UNIQUE EXPERIENCE of traveling to a foreign county. As short-term visitors to a new land, we enjoy the new sights and sounds of the strange yet fascinating travel destination. However, when we are required to stay long-term in a new country, most often we move from an initial fascination with the new culture to a condition commonly termed culture shock. Culture shock occurs when the newness and strangeness of a different culture produces enough stress that we become nearly immobilized.

Culture shock begins to recede when we find a way to get beyond the strangeness and discover the meaning behind the customs of thinking and living in the different culture. Once this kind of connection is made, we can begin to make sense of the surrounding environment and can learn to survive—and even thrive—in the new culture.

For many of us, reading the Bible can be like entering a new country. The culture, language, and customs of both the Old and New Testament can produce in the most dedicated of Bible readers a condition much like the culture shock experienced by visitors to a foreign country. Some of us can become quite "immobilized" in our understanding and application of God's Word. The Bible is indeed new territory for modern readers. Not only are we separated from Bible times by 2,000 to 3,000 years, but we are separated by the major differences inherent between "Western" and "Eastern" ways of thinking. It is easy to say, "I find the people and stories in the Bible so strange. I can't understand them." Or, "The world is so different now. The people in the Bible didn't understand anything about modern science or society. How can the Bible speak to my situation today?"

One of the most important skills we can acquire as Bible readers is the ability to push aside the curtain of cultural detail to discover the essential truth that lies behind it. Separating the interesting, but usually incidental, cultural details from the essential and enduring truth of God's Word requires at least a basic understanding of the Bible's cultural structure. And since God has chosen to work within human history, culture provides the framework from which to explore God's interaction with people.

With this in mind, let's outline 10 cultural differences we encounter in the Bible. A simple understanding of some of these issues will help us in reading God's Word to move beyond the strangeness of an ancient culture so that we can see people who are not that much different from us when it comes to problems, fears, hopes, and ultimately the desire to know and relate to the God of the universe.

Do You Speak the Language?

The most obvious cultural difference between us and the Bible is the language. The original languages of the Bible include Hebrew, Greek, and to a small extent Aramaic (a language very close to Hebrew). Today's Bibles are translations or versions that are based either directly or indirectly on these original languages. Each language has its own ways of giving the reader clues about what is trying to be communicated. Different languages use different ways to ask questions, provide emphasis, introduce new thoughts. Understanding these clues helps us as readers know the true intent of the biblical writer.

For instance, when a prophet uses the phrase "thus says the Lord," we know that he is speaking not on his own authority but on behalf of God. In the New Testament, when Jesus says something He wanted His listeners to really hear, often the phrase "Truly, truly" or "Verily, verily" (in Greek, "amen, amen") introduces it. When we read an opening phrase such as "Grace and peace to you from God our Father and the Lord Jesus Christ" in one of the New Testament books, we know immediately we are reading a letter from the first century.

Names of people and places are especially important in the Hebrew language. Names had meanings attached to them that were well understood by the people of the time but quite often are missed completely by the modern reader. A person's name often said something about his or her character or personality. The name Isaac means "he laughs," reminding us of Abraham and Sarah's laughter when told she would bear a son in her old age. Jacob means "one who takes by the heel," denoting his actions at birth and, not surprisingly, later as an adult. Esau means "hairy," both a characteristic at birth and a part of the drama of his encounter with Jacob later. Isaiah gave one of his children the formidable name Maher-shalal-hashbaz, meaning "the spoil speeds, the prey hastens," signifying the speedy destruction by the Assyrian king. God himself gave His name as Yahweh, "I am." Names that end in a -jah or -el suffix usually include "God" as part of their name meaning. Elijah means "my God is Yahweh"; Nathaniel means "God has given."

Similarly the name of a place often signified the importance of that site. Bethlehem means "house of bread"; Carmel means "garden land." When the angel comforted Hagar near a well in the wilderness, Hagar named the place Beer-lahai-roi, meaning "the well of the living one who sees me."

The language of the Bible is filled with a wide variety of figures of speech that give it richness and color. Simile, hyperbole, foreshadowing, parable, rhetorical questions, poetry, songs, and humor all find their way into God's Word. The key is to recognize these forms of speech and to interpret them appropriately. For example, the psalms often employ a technique called parallelism where one phrase is followed by a second phrase that repeats the theme of the first, but in different words. Psalm 24:1-3 states:

The earth is the LORD's, and everything in it,
   the world, and all who live in it;
for he has founded it upon the seas
   and established it upon the waters.
Who may ascend the hill of the LORD?
   Who may stand in his holy place?

The careful reader will see that lines 2, 4, and 6 do not offer new insights; they merely repeat the idea of the preceding line.

It is interesting that the form of Hebrew and Greek used in the Bible was far from some kind of formal or sacred language. In both cases, the language of the common person, the so-called language of the street, was used. God's written Word meets us at the level of typical human life, just as God's Son came to meet the people of the world in a nondescript manger.

You Can Take My Word for It

Imagine we lived in a society with no television, no radio, no computers, no books, no pens, pencils, or notepads. How would we go about the job of communicating to other people? Simple. We would use the most basic form of communication known to humans—word of mouth. Simple, maybe. But think of all the limitations we would have in a society where all communication depended solely on the words we spoke.

This kind of scenario is like much of the Bible world. We have a hard time imagining a world that does not depend on the written word, but the biblical era, especially in the earliest periods, did not have easy access to writing tools. So communication rested primarily on the spoken word. Because of this fact, a person's word was powerful and binding. We can see the powerful binding effects of the spoken word in the many verbal episodes found, for example, in the Book of Genesis. A negative example of the power of the spoken word is found in the story of Jephthah, who vowed to sacrifice the first thing that came out of his house. When his own daughter, rather than one of his animals, came out first, his spoken word constrained him to follow through on what he had said he would do.

In an oral society, information about the past also depended on the ability to pass on history, important events, and family trees by word of mouth. The ancient Israelites as well as the Jews of Jesus' time were skilled in the now mostly lost art of storytelling. Large amounts of information were carefully and meticulously committed to memory by the community so future generations could benefit from remembering the past. In Deuteronomy 6:6-7 we read an example of this commitment to verbally transfer the past into the present: "These commandments that I give you today are to be upon your hearts. Impress them on your children. Talk about them when you sit . . . , when you walk . . . , when you lie down and when you get up."

In order to assist in the retelling of large amounts of information, memory devices were employed to help the storytellers. Poetry and songs provided rhyme and meter to assist in remembering a story line. Vivid narratives in easily remembered imagery are scattered throughout the Bible. Notice how often the words "now" or "then" occur in these narratives, giving the impression of living action. Psalm 119 is actually an acrostic where each letter of the Hebrew alphabet heads a new section of thought beginning with that letter. The Scriptures are full of plays on words and repeated phrases or words that to us may look redundant but to the ancient Jews were important memory aids.

Religions, Gods, and Superstition

The world of the Bible was characterized by its emphasis on the supernatural. It is probably safe to say there were no atheists in Bible times. While the Bible affirms a monotheistic beginning to humankind's beliefs, from the earliest narratives in Genesis we see the gods begin to multiply. When the Israelites entered the Promised Land, their greatest danger was never the great armies of the Philistines or the imposing walled cities like Jericho. Their greatest danger was the influence of the pagan religions of the land, most notably worship of Baal, the fertility god. It was this god who demanded living sacrifices of its devotees, which amazingly the Israelites participated in from time to time. The religions and gods of the Egyptians, the Philistines, the Assyrians, the Babylonians, and the Persians all offered their forms of worship and belief to the Jews. The Bible records that often the Jews were seduced by these pagan religions. In fact, much of the Bible is a history of Israel's falling away from the one true God and His persistent calling of them back. The struggle didn't end in New Testament times, either, as the Romans and the Greeks presented competing gods to the early Christians.

The ancient world was full of superstition, plagued by demons and spirits. While learning that God was in control of both their lives and the natural world, the Israelites used what appear to us to be rather superstitious practices on occasion. Saul, before one major battle, resorted to consultation with the witch of Endor and her conjured spirits. We read about the use of Thummim and Urim, a kind of dice that, when rolled, supposedly helped make decisions about the future. (For a time apparently this was an accept-able practice to God.) We read in Numbers 5 about the test for an unfaithful wife: after drinking some "bitter" water, if she was guilty, her abdomen would swell. If she was inno-cent, she would not be affected. In the New Testament, many illness were attributed to the habitation of evil spirits within a person. Casting out demons was a marketable skill in the first century, and that is one of the reasons Jesus was such a sought-after healer.

Of course, the ancient world knew nothing of modern sciences. Their view of the world, for example, consisted of a three-tier universe, with Hades below in shadowy caves and heaven in the clouds that floated above a flat earth.

Noting that the world of the Bible was one where a "religious" atmosphere prevailed, it should be acknowl-edged here that the Bible itself is a "religious" book. This may sound overly obvious, but the point is the Bible was written to address issues from a spiritual perspective. While the Bible contains information about history, geogra-phy, politics, and other science-related topics, none of these areas lie at the heart of its primary function—namely to talk about God and His activity among people.

Who's in Charge?

The Bible is cluttered with the names of rulers, kings, princes, pharaohs, and caesars that parade on and off its pages with amazing regularity. The Bible world was domi-nated by dictatorial rulers who were succeeded either through their untimely death by a usurper or in a timely way by a son. These rulers, even many in Israel, were often ruthless in their demand for allegiance and heavy-handed in the taxation leveled on their people. The kinds of free-doms we experience in democratic societies today was vir-tually unknown in ancient times. That is why the issues of oppression, freedom, and peace are often repeated in the pages of the Bible. And that is why the concept of an all-powerful, fully compassionate Messiah-ruler becomes such a pervasive hope in Israel's culture. The present afflictions were only endurable because of a real hope that, in the not-too-distant future, the King of Kings and Lord of Lords would establish His kingdom forever.

Layers of Laws

For many readers of the Bible, the most difficult sections are concentrated around the Jewish Law and especially the Jewish sacrificial system. The innumerable regulations found in the Pentateuch and the endless debates in the New Testament over the Law are hard for modern eyes and ears to fully appreciate. Knowing the differences between "Pharisees and Sadducees," "priests and Levites," or "temples and synagogues" can become rather confusing for us.

Careful readers of the Bible must pick their way between the details of the dated ceremonial laws of the people of Israel and the enduring moral laws for all people and all times. The Ten Commandments are the greatest example of ancient laws that still have complete relevance. However, we certainly do not feel bound by laws found in the Pentateuch concerning using two different kinds of material in one garment or wearing tassels at the four corners of our robes.

The Jewish Law was given at a particular point of moral and religious development in the history of Israel. Recognizing this fact, we modern readers are urged to look behind the cultural regulations that fill the Bible to see their significance and relevance at that point in time so that we can discover the truth God was trying to offer to them —and to us—today.

Reading about the sacrifices of live animals does not make for easy leisure reading either. In fact, one of the most often used words in the Bible is the word "blood." Some new readers to the Bible have described it as gory and disgusting. However, in the ancient world, sacrifice and blood were nothing new to the average person. Most cultures practiced some form of sacrifice. Our modern senses are repulsed by the thought of the slaughter and burning of animals as offerings to God. In that culture, it made sense; in ours it does not. However, the Jewish sacrificial system does begin to help us appreciate to a greater extent the supreme sacrifice of Jesus Christ for our sins. That sacrifice, too, is repulsive to our modern senses, yet it was the only way for you and me to be offered salvation.

This Land Is My Land

While the Bible mentions many ways that people in the Bible acquired wealth—gold, animals, servants—the undisputed sign of wealth and security was owning land. Land in the Middle Eastern environment was not always in abundant supply. Once you obtained land, either through purchase or by means of force, it was a commodity worth dying for. Land was carefully passed on from father to son. Boundary markers were placed and meticulously watched to ensure that not one acre was lost.

Much of the Bible is concerned with the land. Abraham journeys to a new land. The Israelites conquer the Promised Land. Later the apostate Jews are removed from their land. The land was a sign of God's blessing on the people, from it they produced their harvests, and on it their livestock were fed. The land was the basis for the many festivals and holidays celebrated throughout the Jewish year. The land was life itself. No wonder today the Jews and Palestinians are so insistent that they not give any land away to each other. To give away land is to give away life.

Crossing the Boundaries

How many times have you encountered a name or place in the Bible that was unpronounceable? (And how many times has this happened while reading aloud in a public setting?) Indeed the Bible is filled with names of people and nations strange to us today. The reason so many names are listed in the Bible is found in the fact that the Bible world was one of political turmoil and instability. Because travel was slow and natural barriers abounded in this region, many separate kingdoms could exist in a relatively small geographical area. Today, visitors to the Holy Land are amazed at how compact an area Israel is. Nations and kingdoms, large and small, rose and fell, conquered and surrendered, threatened and disappeared. To us, these territorial transitions are often without meaning. But to the Bible writers, these notes about who was in power and who was not often provide the essential context of the biblical message. The biblical writers assume the readers know the significance of the information they provide. We modern readers may have to work some to understand this context, but the effort is well worth the investment.

The whole Bible story is really based upon the background of political unrest. Three of the Bible's most significant themes—the Exodus from Egypt, the Exile to Babylon, and the Return to Israel under the Persians—have their roots in the story of nations pitted against nations.

Like Father, like Son

In our gender-conscious culture, it may be hard for some to admit that the Bible is largely colored by a male-dominant perspective. The people of the Bible are usually characterized as a patriarchal society, where only men were important. The common prayer of the male Jew was thankfulness for not having been born a Gentile, a dog, or a woman. Birth events were filled with joyful celebration when a boy was born and silent disappointment when it was a girl.

Most of the influential characters in the Bible are noted without apology as men. Most of the genealogies mention only men. To do otherwise would have been a violation of their cultural norms.

That's why when the Bible does occasionally mention women as leaders, as influential in history, as part of a genealogy, we should recognize a major shift in the accepted cultural patterns of the day. When Jesus talked to the Samaritan woman at the well, He was doing something almost unthinkable in that culture. When Paul states in Galatians 3.28 that there is neither Jew nor Greek, slave nor free, male nor female, we know that the culture of the biblical world was being turned upside down.

The Right Thing to Do

One of the more misunderstood topics of the Old Testament is the subject of ethics and morals. We read of people like Abraham who married his half-sister; Onan who refused to help his sister-in-law have a child and thus was slain by God; Solomon who had 700 wives; and Jeremiah who lied to save the king's life. We read about a wide variety of offenses that carried a capital punishment with it, often in seemingly cruel ways. We read of apparently innocent children being killed. We are told that an eye for an eye was suitable behavior. These ethical standards do not always match civilized, much less Christian, standards today.

The reader must keep in mind several facts when reading the Old Testament from an ethical point of view. First, not all examples given in the Old Testament are meant to be positive examples. Abraham's decision to lie to Pharaoh about his wife, Sarah, failed in its intended purpose and surely was contrary to God's will. While Abraham and Sarah's decision to have an heir through Sarah's servant Hagar was completely in accord with the customs of the day, they preempted God's better plan. Second, the Israelites were learning, sometimes slowly, how to love God and love their neighbor. No one, including God, expected them to move from virtual paganism to the kind of ethics later taught by Jesus all at once. Scholars have called this development process "progressive revelation." God provided light on the truth a little at a time and expected His people to walk in all the light they understood. In other words, God worked within their cultural mind-set and began to move them forward. Third, in spite of some of the less than Christian responses we read in the Old Testament, we have to remember that quite often the Israelites' behavior was far ahead of their pagan neighbors and the world at that time. The world of the Bible was a place where life and death came in sudden bursts. The ancient Jews tried to at least recognize the value of life and to curb the excesses of untimely death. Fourth, the New Testament builds on the ethical foundations outlined in the Old Testament and brings them to fulfillment. An "eye for an eye" is replaced by "love your enemies" (Matthew 5:38-44). "You shall not murder" is enhanced to "do not be angry with your brother or sister" (see vv. 21-22). The great ethical truths of God are provided for us in His Word; sometimes, however, we must push aside the cultural curtain to discover their full application.

Much of the Bible is dedicated to issues of fairness. The poor, the downtrodden, the widow, the unfortunate, the weak are all declared to be under the protection of the people and of God. Ethics in the Bible is not some theoretical discussion saved for the courtroom. Ethics is something important that affects the day-to-day life of one's neighbor.

Ultimately, the call to ethical lifestyle is summed up in the call of God to "be holy, because I am holy" (Leviticus 11:44). The Bible knows no greater moral goal than to be like God.

It All Happened So Fast

Finally, remember that the events in the Bible, though compressed in the pages of our Bible, actually took place over decades and centuries of time. What we are given in

God's Word are only the highlights of biblical history. Within a few verses we can jump several generations of time. What seems like a short story really is the entire history of a people.

During this long period of time, the characters we encounter in the Bible developed and changed. The Jews we read about in the Gospels are not exactly the same as the Jews we read about in the Book of Joshua. Over a period of 1,000 years people change, grow, develop. Think about the differences between us and persons who lived 1,000 years ago. We differ in our ideas, issues we consider important, and even the language we speak. Looking only 100 years ago, we can see rapid changes that have occurred. While societal change in the biblical era did not happen as quickly as it does today, we can begin to get a feel for the potential differences in ideas, emphases, and language that can occur over the great time frame of the Bible.

Conclusion

Recognizing the many cultural uniquenesses in the Bible and moving beyond them may sound like an imposing job for the average Bible reader. In fact, some scholars have committed their entire lives and careers to this goal. However, for you and me it is often enough to simply understand that there is a cultural curtain to push aside and to begin finding ways to recognize some of the basics of biblical culture. This process is not as hard as it may seem. Small amounts of time invested in this kind of education certainly are rewarding and make Bible reading richer and fuller.

The key to understanding the Bible in all its cultural robes is to recognize, after all is said and done, that people are people and God is God. The call to become a member of the people of God is the same today as it was when God first called Abraham in a faraway place and a long-ago time.

Background Scripture: Leviticus 11:44; Deuteronomy 6:6-7; Psalm 24:1-3; Matthew 5:21-22, 38-44; Galatians 3:28

Memory Verses: Psalm 139:23-24

Randy Cloud is director of Adult Ministries for the Church of the Nazarene in Kansas City, Missouri.

5

Seven Keys to Understanding Scripture

by Tremper Longman III

SUPPOSE YOU FIND A LETTER with no return address in your mailbox. It reads: "Don't worry. The bills are on the way." Would you understand what it means?

College students might think they know immediately what such a message means. "The bills" are money from home—like 10s and 20s. The sender is a parent or rich relative, bailing the student out of some financial disaster.

But what if the message is from the car repair shop, and "the bills" are the kind you have to pay? What if a devious little sister wrote the note as a joke? What if "the bills" are your Cousin Bill and your Uncle Bill coming to spend the weekend?

How easy it is to misunderstand. The context of the message and the perspective of the receiver make all the difference in the world. Imagine the surprised look on the college student's face when "the bills" arrive, and they are not the kind you can spend.*

Just as we might miss the meaning of a letter, we can also miss the message of the Bible. Because the Bible is such a special book we sometimes forget this. Yet, everyone who reads the Bible interprets the text. Unfortunately, however, the Bible is not always easy to understand. Even when the text seems straightforward, we may feel uncertain that our interpretation is right. All of us want to treat the Word of God with the respect it deserves, and we certainly don't want to read into it things that are not there. For these reasons, we need to apply the basic principles of hermeneutics (her-meh-NEW-tiks)—the science of interpretation—as we read the text.

Many believers already apply these principles just by using common sense. Indeed, they are simply principles of good reading. Though the Bible is a unique book in many ways, many of the rules for interpreting the Bible are rules for interpreting any book.

The goal of our Bible reading and study is to find out what the Bible means. These seven principles can help us understand what God is saying to us through Scripture.

Principle 1: Look for the author's intended meaning.

Notice that this principle acknowledges that there *is* a meaning to the text. In an age of relativism, this point is important. Many non-Christian interpreters of the Bible suggest that the Bible has no set meaning, and we may read into it whatever we want. On the contrary, we must realize that, when we interpret the Bible, we are looking for the author's original meaning, not imposing our own meaning on a text. When the reader's interpretation conflicts with the author's, then the reader is wrong.

Each biblical passage has a set meaning intended by its author. The interpreter's task is to discover that meaning. This principle seems clear enough, but we must come to grips with a couple of issues.

First, who is the author and how do we uncover his intention? This question is more complex than it might first appear. Even when we know the name of the human author (Moses, Paul, etc.), we have no independent access to him. We can't ask Paul whether he was describing Christians or non-Christians in Romans 7:21-25. We can only answer such questions by placing ourselves in the time period when the authors first wrote and asking what they meant to tell us (see Principle 4).

A second issue has to do with the unique character of the Bible as the Word of God. As 2 Peter 1:21 states, "Prophecy never had its origin in the will of man, but men spoke from God as they were carried along by the Holy Spirit." God is the ultimate Author of the Bible, and this important truth has implications for how we understand it.

Let's look at an example, "When Israel was a child, I loved him, and out of Egypt I called my son" (Hosea 11:1).

Who is the author of this passage? According to the first verse of Hosea, it is the prophet by that name. But how can we know what his intention is in the passage? First, we know approximately when he lived. We also have the broader context of the whole book, which gives us a fuller idea of what Hosea intended to say in this one verse. When we study his text in the context of his entire book, we find that Hosea is referring to the Exodus described in the Book of Exodus.

But later we may be reading Matthew 2 and come across verse 15. Here the writer applies Hosea 11:1 to Jesus as a youth returning to Judea from Egypt. This reference does not seem in keeping with the intention of Hosea. It is here we must remember where the meaning of a text ultimately resides—in the intention of its Author, God himself. And as we read the scripture in the context of the Bible as a whole, we see that He has made an analogy between Israel, God's children, being freed from Egypt and Jesus, God's Son, coming up from Egypt, a pattern that runs throughout Matthew's Gospel.

Principle 2: Read a passage in context.

With the Bible, as with all good literature, we must get a grasp of the whole in order to appreciate and understand the parts. This principle doesn't stop us from turning to the middle of the Book of Romans to read a section on sin, but we should only do so with an understanding of where Paul's teaching on sin fits in with the message of the whole book.

When we do read little bits and pieces of Scripture, we must exercise great caution. Imagine reading Paul's words in 1 Corinthians 7:27: "Are you unmarried? Do not look for a wife." Without taking into account the context, especially Paul's advice in verse 9, we might conclude that the Bible commands celibacy.

Context is an ever-expanding concept when applied to a passage of scripture. For example, take Genesis 50:20, where Joseph says, "You intended to harm me, but God intended it for good to accomplish what is now being done, the saving of many lives." If we look at the immediate context, we will see that he is speaking to his brothers right after his father died. To understand what he is referring to we need to read the entire Joseph story (37:1—50:26). Here we see that his brothers tried to get rid of him by selling him to Midianite traders, who took him to Egypt. We also observe how God used their evil actions to place him in a position of power from which he could save his family.

But even further, we have to read Genesis 50:20 in the light of the whole Book of Genesis. Genesis describes the promise that God gave Abraham about numerous descendants and land. Joseph's statement at the end of the book shows his awareness that God is overruling the evil of his brothers' intentions in order to preserve the family line and fulfill His promise to Abraham.

And we are still not done. The ultimate context of any Bible passage is the whole Bible. As we read the Bible, we see many parallels to Joseph's statement, but none so vivid as the words of Peter as he describes Jesus' death. In Acts 2:22-24 Peter says that Jesus was killed by men who only intended to kill Him, but God used those very actions to save many from their sins.

How do we learn to read in context? Avoid only reading little snippets of scripture. Read whole books. If you can sit down for two or three hours to read a novel, try the same with Isaiah or Acts. Whenever you do read a short passage, do it with an outline of the whole book in your mind or with the help of a good commentary.

Of course, the exact nature of the context may differ from book to book in the Bible. The context of the historical books is provided by the flow of events of the story. In the letters, one idea comes from another. Proverbs 10—31 has a looser context as one pithy proverb on laziness is followed by two on the tongue and then another on laziness. Still, in all books we should have a sense of the whole book as we study any part of it. Ask, how does this passage fit into the message of the whole book, even the whole Bible?

Our ability to read the Scriptures in their ever-expanding context will increase the more we spend time reading God's Word.

Principle 3: Identify the type of the passage you are reading.

One evening I opened a new book and was jarred by this opening sentence: "As Gregor Samsa awoke from an uneasy sleep, he found himself transformed into a gigantic insect." It was a striking sentence, but it didn't shake me. The book was *Metamorphosis* by Franz Kafka, a fictional story in which human beings can turn into bugs without raising the reader's disbelief.

The Bible is a cornucopia of literary types. As we read from Genesis to Revelation we encounter history, poetry, prophecy, proverb, gospel, parable, epistle, and apocalypse. Knowing the type of literature you are reading is essential to understanding it. Different types evoke different expectations and interpretive strategies.

Let's take as a classic example a book of the Bible that has been misinterpreted because its literary type was misidentified. For a long time, the Song of Songs was interpreted as an allegory of the relationship between Jesus Christ and the Church. When early interpreter Cyril of Alexandria read Song of Songs 1:13, "My lover is to me a sachet of myrrh resting between my breasts," he thought the two breasts represented the Old and New Testaments. The sachet was Christ, who spanned both!

Most people today recognize that the Song is a love poem. Its primary message concerns the intimacy of human love. Of course, since human love reflects Christ's love for the Church (see Ephesians 5:22-32), the older interpreters were not entirely wrong. Yet they did miss the most obvious meaning of the text.

Principle 4: Consider the historical and cultural background of the Bible.

The Bible was written in a time far distant from ours and in cultures quite strange to us. So as we try to discover the author's meaning, we must learn to read his writing as one of his contemporaries would. We must transport ourselves by means of our informed imagination back to the time of Moses, David, Solomon, or Paul.

How do we do this? For most Bible readers, it means turning to commentaries and other helps. These books can give us insight into the cultural and historical backgrounds to the biblical books.

For instance, the Bible often depicts the Lord as riding a cloud (Psalms 18:7-15; 68:4; 104:3; Nahum 1:3). We might learn from a commentary that Israel's neighbors frequently pictured the god Baal riding a cloud chariot into battle. As we place the biblical image in the light of the ancient Near East, we realize that God's cloud is a chariot that He rides into war. When we turn to the New Testament and see that Jesus also is a cloud rider (Matthew 24:30; Revelation 1:7), we understand that this is not a white, fluffy cloud but a storm cloud that He rides into judgment. Furthermore, we now sense that the use of the image was an appeal to those Israelites who worshiped the wrong god, Baal, to come back and worship the true cloud rider, the Lord.

But what about a passage like Psalm 23? Can't we understand the imagery of a shepherd without recourse to the ancient world? We know what a shepherd does. He protects, guides, and takes care of his sheep.

The answer is yes and no. Shepherds in biblical times acted like shepherds in modern times in all these ways. However, unless we are aware of the use of the shepherd image in the ancient Near East, we will miss an important aspect of the psalm. The great kings of the Near East often referred to themselves as the "shepherds" of their people. Thus, as we read Psalm 23 in the light of its ancient background, we recover an important teaching of Psalm 23: the Lord is a royal shepherd.

Principle 5: Consider the grammar and structure within the passage.

In other words, we must read our passage closely in all its detail. Look for things like connectors, verb tenses, and modifiers to nouns. Connectors (words like "but," "and," "therefore"), for instance, help give the reader the logical connection between words. Remember, though, that the meaning of the Bible is not in the isolated words. Meaning is in the context, namely, in sentences.

Let's look at the conjunctions, tense, adjectives, and other indications of the relationship between words and clauses in Psalm 131.

Our example comes from a poem that has a special kind of structural feature, parallelism, in which the clauses echo each other. The first clause makes a statement, which is then expanded upon in the following related clauses. When reading a poem, reflect on how the parallelism contributes to the meaning of the psalm.

The parallel structure (both in the meaning of the

words and the grammar) links the first three clauses of verse 1 together:

My heart is not proud, O LORD,
  my eyes are not haughty;
I do not concern myself with great matters
  or things too wonderful for me.

Careful attention to the structural relationship between the three clauses shows that David distances himself from pride in three distinct areas: his core personality (heart), his external demeanor (eyes), and his actions.

The "but" that begins the second verse draws a strong contrast between the pride described in the first verse and the attitude expressed in the second.

But I have stilled and quieted my soul;
  like a weaned child with its mother,
  like a weaned child is my soul within me.

The English translation of the Hebrew verbs ("have stilled" and "have quieted") indicate that his confidence is rooted in the past and continues in the present.

He then illustrates his present disposition by using the word "like." Note that David does not use a generic term for child but the word for a weaned child. When we reflect on the word choice, we may realize that a weaned child, one that does not need its mother's milk, is especially calm in its mother's lap. It is not grasping for the source of its sustenance but resting quietly in its mother's arms.

The final verse of the psalm uses imperatives in order to drive home the application of the truths presented in the first two verses:

O Israel, put your hope in the LORD
  both now and forevermore.

Principle 6: Interpret experience in the light of Scripture, not Scripture in the light of experience.

All too often, we distort Scripture by allowing our experience to shape our understanding of Scripture rather than the other way around.

One way we let experience dictate our interpretation is by imposing our desires upon it. Many believers find a passage out of context to support their desire, ignore the rest of the Bible's teaching, and argue that their desire is the same as biblical truth.

For instance, if sharing my faith made me uncomfortable, I might build an excuse for not doing evangelism around scriptures about God's love. I could quote 1 Corinthians 13 and a host of other passages to show that God and love are nearly synonymous. Then I might reason: "If God is love, how could He condemn anybody?" In this way, I would be off the hook for telling people about Jesus despite all the clear teaching about sin, judgment, and hell.

Another way that experience can warp our interpretation of Scripture is through our cultural makeup. We can unconsciously make the Bible a modern political text as we read into it the values that come naturally to us due to our upbringing. Capitalism is nowhere taught as such in Scripture, socialism isn't either. Yet North American right-wing Christians and Latin American proponents of liberation theology both use the Bible to promote their agendas. The antidote to such lopsided readings is to also study biblical passages that undermine both capitalism and socialism. Our experience of one system or the other should not figure into considering one philosophy biblical and the other unbiblical.

Principle 7: Always seek the full counsel of Scripture.

We should never read Scripture in isolation from the whole Bible. While many human authors contributed to the Bible, God is the Ultimate Author of the whole. While the Bible is an anthology of many books, it is also one Book. While it has many stories to tell, they all contribute to a single Story.

This principle has many important implications. First, we should never base doctrine or moral teaching of Scripture on an obscure passage. The most important ideas in the Bible are stated more than once. When a text teaches something obscure or difficult and we can find no other passage to support it, we must not attach too much significance to it.

Second, if one passage *seems* to teach something, but another passage clearly teaches something else, we must understand the former in terms of the latter. That is, we must determine the meaning of the unclear verse by examining the clear teaching of Scripture.

Not long ago I was asked to debate a popular radio teacher on the subject of Christ's return. The teacher had just published a lengthy book arguing that Jesus was going to come again in a specific year.

The debate never would have happened if he and his supporters had simply applied this principle. You see, they had all kinds of convoluted, mathematical arguments based on obscure interpretations of Scripture that led them to believe that Christ would return in that year. But the clear teaching of Scripture refutes the teacher's arguments. Take a look at Mark 13:32: "No one knows about that day or hour." Just reading that clear verse should have stopped all the stretching and manipulating of passages to reach a conclusion.

In order to grasp the full counsel of Scripture, we need to study the themes and analogies that stretch from Genesis to Revelation. Then, when we read any one passage, we will be able to understand its place in the unfolding history of salvation.

This principle is particularly important as we read the Old Testament. After all, Jesus himself told us that the whole Old Testament, not just a handful of messianic prophecies, looks forward to His coming (see Luke 24:25-27, 44).

Take as an example Matthew 4:1-11, which describes

Jesus' temptation in the wilderness. If we keep the whole of Scripture in mind as we read, we may pick up signals when we read that Jesus, the Son of God, spent 40 days and 40 nights in the wilderness. This reference may remind us of the Israelites' 40-year trek in the wilderness. But the comparison goes beyond the number 40. The Israelites also were tempted in the wilderness in the same three areas in which Jesus was tempted: (1) hunger and thirst, (2) testing God, and (3) worshiping false gods. Jesus, however, shows himself to be the obedient Son of God where the Israelites were disobedient. Indeed, Jesus responded to the temptations by quoting Deuteronomy, the sermon that Moses gave the Israelites at the end of their 40-year sojourn.

Reading Scripture in the light of the whole message, the whole counsel of God, not only prevents erroneous interpretations but also gives us deeper insight into the Word of God.

Conclusion

It is impossible to approach the Bible in a completely objective way. We all come to the Bible with questions, issues, troubles, and joys. Each of us also approaches the Bible from different cultural and social experiences. This truth contains great benefit and danger.

The benefit is that the Bible is relevant for every life. The danger, of course, is that we will warp God's Word in a way that it was never intended to be read.

There are three ways to avoid the danger while maximizing the benefits. The first is to follow the seven principles for understanding Scripture. These can keep us from reading our own thoughts into the Bible and help us discover the intention of the Author himself.

The second is to read the Bible in community. That is, don't be a "Lone Ranger" in Bible interpretation. Talk to others about what the Bible means to them and be open to their reading of the text. Read books by Christians from other walks of life and different cultural backgrounds.

Finally, bathe your Scripture reading in prayer and ask the Holy Spirit to open your eyes to the truth found in the Word. Without the Spirit we cannot understand God's Word (see 1 Corinthians 2:6-16).

Understanding Scripture does not have to be a daunting task. After all, the God who gave us His Word longs for us to understand it even more than we do.

Background Scripture: Genesis 37:1—50:26; Psalms 18:7-15; 23:1-6; 68:4; 104:3; 131:1-3; Proverbs 10—31; Song of Songs 1:13; Hosea 11:1; Matthew 2:15; 4:1-11; 24:30; Mark 13:32; Luke 24:25-27, 44; Acts 2:22-24; Romans 7:21-25; 1 Corinthians 2:6-16; 7:27; 13:1-13; Ephesians 5:22-32; 2 Peter 1:21; Revelation 1:7

Memory Verse: Luke 11:28

Dr. Tremper Longman III is a professor and chair of the Old Testament department at Westminster Theological Seminary in Philadelphia, Pennsylvania.

---

*The opening illustration was supplied by Dr. James Edlin, professor of biblical literature and language at MidAmerica Nazarene College, Olathe, Kansas.

6

Is Jesus a Thief?

by Lance Hartman

MOST EVANGELICALS AGREE that it's best to interpret Scripture literally. But what exactly does this mean? Some have applied a literal interpretation to Matthew 5:29: "If your right eye causes you to sin, gouge it out and throw it away," only to discover that lust requires neither eye nor hand. Should literal interpretation have limitations? If so, what are they?

"Literal" is probably not the best choice of terms to describe what is meant by taking the Scriptures at face value. Indeed, if we say, "It's raining cats and dogs outside," only an extreme literalist would look for felines and canines. By ignoring the normal rules of language, history, and culture, even clearly figurative constructions are taken literally by some people. When Jesus called Herod a "fox," normal rules of language force us to search for valid points of comparison and not to literally view Herod as a furry, four-legged animal. In a similar way, if we hear someone refer to a person as being an "iceberg," few of us would look for an actual block of ice. We know that the speaker is commenting by use of a figure of speech on that person's coldness.

What then does it mean to properly interpret the Scriptures literally? It means to understand the writer's original intended meaning based upon the normal and proper use of language customary for that day, paying close attention to the context of the words. This definition can also apply to interpreting all the figurative language found in the Bible. We interpret figures, not based on the literal words but on the author's literal intent lying behind the figures. For instance, Jesus spoke figuratively in John 6:35 saying, "I am the bread of life." To interpret this literally, we look past the literal meaning of the word "bread" and seek the characteristic of bread that Jesus intended His hearers to understand. Thus the literal meaning is not that Jesus was a loaf but that just as bread sustains physical life, He is essential to sustain spiritual life. The literal intent had to do with the idea of His necessity for our lives.

Words acquire new meanings with the passage of time and usage in various contexts. The process of literal interpretation takes this into consideration. Notice the word "gay." An article mentioning a "gay march" requires us to know the context and the time period of the statement to determine meaning. If written in the 1950s, we could be almost certain that "gay" was describing the excitement of the march. The context of the article would confirm this. However, a 1990s article would just as certainly be referring to the sexual orientation of the participants, which can be confirmed by context. The phrase "good Samaritan" represents today one who is charitable, but to Jesus' Jewish audience there could be no such thing as a *good* Samaritan. As despised half-breeds, Samaritans could do no "good." To miss the historical setting that gives the word "Samaritan" its special force is to miss Jesus' intent and to cloud our contemporary search for applications.

Proper literal interpretation requires observing several guidelines:

Word Meanings. First, attempt to understand the range of meanings that words had in ancient times. Bible dictionaries will help here. Then see which meaning works best in the context. For instance, compare the different meanings of "flesh" in Matthew 19:5; John 1:14; and Romans 8:13 (translated by the NIV as "sinful nature").

Type.[1] Second, observe the type of writing. Is it poetry? Historical narrative? Prophecy? Letter? Different forms communicate meaning in distinct ways.

Figures. Third, seek the literal intent of figurative language. As a general rule, if a statement would be absurd on a literal level, interpret it as a figure. Establish the relevant point of comparison of the figure and interpret the author's original intention.

Context. Fourth, always interpret a text in a way that makes the most sense in its own context. We all speak and think in connected thoughts and dislike having our words taken out of context. We should not expect less from the inspired authors of the Bible. A text considered in its context yields the author's literal intent. This becomes increasingly important when we realize that authors use identical words differently in various contexts. This explains the distinction between Paul and James concerning faith and works. They employ the same words differently, as the contexts demonstrate.

Signs of the Times. Fifth, observe how the immediate historical (events) and cultural (customs) setting of a text impacts its intended meaning. For instance, does 1 Corinthians 11:5 mean that a woman had better have a hat on to pray? Do foot washing ceremonies have the same meaning in contemporary society as in John 13:5?

Meaning Before Application. Finally, distinguish the author's intended meaning (usually singular) from the possible applications. The literal method of interpretation has to do with what the Bible is saying. Armed with the author's original intent, we are better prepared to make valid applications that will be consistent with the intended meaning. We interpret the unchanging Word of God before we apply it to our ever-changing world. We will discuss this idea more fully in chapter 8.

Above all, keep in mind that the biblical authors and the God who inspired them used language with the intent to be understood. This is the underlying premise to the literal method of interpretation. When the plain sense of Scripture makes good sense, we should seek no other sense. As John Wesley once said, "The general rule of interpreting Scripture is this: the literal sense of every text is to be taken, if it be not contrary to some other texts; but in that case the obscure text is to be interpreted by those which speak more plainly."[2]

The plain sense of any scripture passage often lies within rich and evocative phrases. Language is God's handiwork. Those He inspired to write the Scriptures—from Moses and the prophets to Paul, Peter, and John—became language masters. Often, God led them to use literary techniques to communicate His Word. One of the most common of these techniques is figures of speech. Found in all literature, figures of speech have been called the "ornaments of language." They allow the author to transform a simple, literal idea into a clearer, more graphic image for the reader. Let's take a look at some of the most frequently used figures of speech in the Bible.

Figures of Comparison

A *simile* (SIH-mih-lee) is a comparison in which something is said to be "like" or "as" another thing. For example, "As the deer pants for streams of water, so my soul pants for you, O God" (Psalm 42:1).

A *metaphor* (MEH-tah-for) is a comparison in which it is said that something "is" another thing. For example, "Your word is a lamp to my feet and a light for my path" (Psalm 119:105).

Similes and metaphors force us to stop and consider how one thing compares with another. How is the longing of our souls like the longings of a deer? In what ways is God's Word a lamp and a light? Once we see what they share in common, we will understand what God is saying to us.

We must be careful not to press the comparisons too far, beyond what they could have meant to the original audience. It would be wrong to conclude from Revelation 16:15 that Jesus is a thief. When He said, "Behold, I come like a thief!" the point of comparison is that of unexpectedness, not questionable character. In comparing Christians to salt in Matthew 5:13, Jesus did not have every contemporary use of salt in mind. In ancient times, salt was not used to deice roads. Thus it would be incorrect to say that one meaning is that Christians are to melt people's coldheartedness toward God.

As with all interpretation, immediate context is our surest safeguard. Notice that Revelation 16:15 is in a context of alertness and readiness in the midst of turmoil. Knowing that Jesus could come any moment, as unexpectedly as a thief, believers are never to relax their faithfulness. The salt metaphor, like its corollary of light, comes on the heels of the beatitudes, which describe the countercultural attitudes of believers. However, we are not to step out of our culture but to be change agents within our culture, preserving what is good and demonstrating by our lives the reality of God.

Figures that Intensify

Hyperbole (high-PER-bow-lee) is an intentional exaggeration or overstatement designed to achieve an emotional effect. Here are two examples: "If anyone comes to me and does not hate his father and mother, his wife and children, his brothers and sisters—yes, even his own life—he cannot be my disciple" (Luke 14:26). "So the Pharisees said to one another, 'See, this is getting us nowhere. Look how the whole world has gone after him!'" (John 12:19).

The use of hyperbole is more common than we may think. We have all said something like, "I wrote until my hand fell off!" or "My feet are killing me!" While hands do not fall off and rarely do people drop dead from aching feet, hyperbole is a way of expressing the emotional truth about something. It describes the way it *feels* to us. It is also a way of abruptly getting another's attention. The examples above illustrate both purposes.

Jesus' words in Luke 14:26 seem extreme. That should alert us to the use of hyperbole. If we took these words literally, they would contradict the abundant biblical teaching on honoring one's parents and loving all people (even enemies), not to mention the teachings against hate (see 1 John 4:20). This is an example of Jesus driving home a point in a way that forces us to take note of it. With further reflection, we realize that Jesus is saying that love for Him should take precedence over all other affections and allegiances, making them seem like "hate" by comparison.

The Pharisees in John 12:19 show us hyperbole to express a strong feeling—exasperation. It would be nice if the whole world was going after Jesus, but this has never been the case—then or now. However, if we were Pharisees in A.D. 30 watching crowds flocking around Jesus, it might have felt as if everyone was abandoning us in favor of Jesus. The Pharisees were frustrated at the loss of their influence over the people.

The key to interpreting hyperbole is never to take it literally but to look for the ways in which it is either expressing what is emotionally true or serving to grab our attention. Yet before we tame a saying too much, we should wrestle with how radical Jesus' teachings really are.

Figures of Contrast

Irony is a way of intentionally saying the opposite of what is meant. For example, "As for you, O house of Israel, this is what the Sovereign LORD says: Go and serve your idols, every one of you!" (Ezekiel 20:39). Or "Already you have all you want! Already you have become rich!" (1 Corinthians 4:8).

Here is another figure of speech that should be familiar to us. You might be asked, "How was the meeting with your boss?" and answer sarcastically, "Can't wait till the next one!" This is irony. It is easy to pick up in a conversation because intonation tips us off. However we must be more alert to catch it in the written text. Irony is used, not to hide meaning, but to add greater force and vividness. I'm not likely to mistake your meaning as wanting to meet with your boss again, but using irony says it more vividly.

In Ezekiel 20:39, God is surely not commanding His people to break the second commandment and worship other gods. Rather, as the context points out, Israel is already doing this. God really wants them to worship Him. He is allowing Israel to go on their chosen path, promising the discipline of judgment. He works in the same way today.

In a similar way, Paul uses irony to address spiritual pride in Corinth, saying the opposite of what he really thinks to be true. Far from being a commendation, 1 Corinthians 4:8 condemns the Corinthians' false self-perceptions. They thought they had arrived spiritually. By using irony, Paul portrays their folly more vividly and forcefully. He knows that neither he nor they—nor any of us this side of eternity—can claim we have no more room for growth. There is no place for spiritual pride in our lives.

In the Bible, irony is usually found in situations of rebuke or ridicule. Often there is an intent to censure or criticize concealed in an ironic statement. As the context will always show, irony cannot be true if taken at face value. It is the opposite meaning that the author wants to convey.

Figures of Association

Metonymy (meh-TAH-neh-mee) is substituting one thing for another closely related to it. For example, "Now, therefore, the sword will never depart from your house, because you despised me and took the wife of Uriah the Hittite to be your own" (2 Samuel 12:10).

Synecdoche (si-NEK-doh-kee) is where one part is substituted for the whole or the whole for a part. An example is, "They will beat their swords into plowshares and their spears into pruning hooks" (Isaiah 2:4). Another example is, "Their destiny is destruction, their god is their stomach" (Philippians 3:19).

While the names may be unfamiliar, these, too, are figures we use fairly often. We might say, "I don't agree with anything the White House is doing," referring to the president and his staff. Or we may speak of a friend being ruined by "the bottle," by which we mean drunkenness. These are both examples of metonymy. Similarly, we might read that the city imposed a curfew on children under 18. Here, "city" refers to the government, not the entire town.

When we come across metonymy, we should pause to ask ourselves why the writer chose to say things this way. What do the images suggest? Don't make the mistake of interpreting too narrowly or literally.

In 2 Samuel 12:10, the prophet Nathan was not telling David that he would always have a sword in his house. Rather, "sword" is associated with violence and "house" refers to David's family. Because he had sown seeds of violence against the innocent Uriah, violence would plague David and his family. However, the word "sword" conjures up a more vivid image, and the use of "house" indicates the pervasive consequences of David's sin. How wide a circle the influence of one person's sin can become!

Coming to our examples of synecdoche, Isaiah was not reducing the Israelites to fighting with slingshots and bows and arrows. By mentioning a part, swords and spears, he was using synecdoche to refer to all instruments of war. There was coming a day of total disarmament.

In Philippians 3:19, Paul refers to the enemies of Christianity as those whose god is their stomach. Do they really worship their stomachs? This is a use of synecdoche, so we must look for an association. We typically associate the stomach with appetite. Paul intends this to represent all the fruitless appetites of a life lived in the flesh and not in the Spirit. Consider, though, how readily we can all identify through the word "stomach" with a vivid image of cravings.

Conclusion

The Bible is indeed the inspired Word of God. We can more fully appreciate its meaning because God chose so many ornaments—figures of speech—by which to communicate His truth. The Bible is not dry; it uses language that causes vivid images to pop into our minds. The more we contemplate the meaning of these images, the greater will be our appreciation of God's Word, and the better prepared we will be to apply it to our lives.

Background Scripture: 2 Samuel 12:10; Psalms 42:1; 119:105; Isaiah 2:4; Ezekiel 20:39; Matthew 5:13, 29; 19:5; Luke 14:26; John 1:14; 6:35; 12:19; 13:5; Romans 8:13; 1 Corinthians 4:8; 11:5; Philippians 3:19; 1 John 4:20; Revelation 16:15

Memory Verse: Hebrews 4:12

Lance Hartman is an adjunct professor at both Colorado Christian University and Denver Seminary, and he pastors a church in Colorado Springs, Colorado.

---

1. The term often used to describe a type of literature is "genre" (JAHN-ruh).
2. John Telford, *The Letters of the Rev. John Wesley, A.M.* (London: Epworth Press, 1931), 129.

7

Variety Is the Spice

by Peggy Poteet

"I DON'T LIKE TO READ THE BIBLE. It's so boring—all those 'begats' and 'thou shalt nots.' It puts me to sleep."

"I try to read it, but there is a lot that I just don't understand."

"The Bible is simple. Just take it all at face value. Every part is the same. Even a child can read it."

"How can we really understand the Scriptures without reading them in the original languages?"

"It's Greek to me!"

Could one of those statements be ours? Do we read the Bible just because we must? Do we read only certain parts and ignore the rest? Do we pick it up expecting to be bored? Do we sometimes wish we could just watch it on video?

Look again.

It's in There

All human experience is in there—anything that could ever happen to us. It confronts us straight on—honestly, explicitly, concretely. It makes us laugh, cry, or feel comfort or shame. It can raise the hair on our necks or challenge our imaginations with fantastic pictures of the end of time. It is God's message made flesh in an infinite variety of forms, and it is written just for us.

From the joys of love in Song of Songs to the shame of adultery in the story of David and Bathsheba. From the common sibling rivalry of Adam's descendants to the profound friendship of David and Jonathan. From the mystery of the presence of God on Mount Sinai to the reality of mundane life in a barren desert. From the dusty streets of Nazareth and the common men who followed Jesus to the fantastic visions of Daniel and John. A multitude of life experiences in a multitude of forms appear on the Bible's pages.

This Is Better than TV

The Bible stories could make for some great television channels. For example . . .

History Channel: Shepherd boy rises to political heights amid court intrigue and family rivalry.

Bible Arts Network: Lyric poetry from lament to praise; beautiful sounds from harps and timbrels.

Paul-Silas Headline News: Latest report of missionary activity in Eastern Europe and the Middle East.

Travel Network: Would-be big-time evangelist swallowed by large fish on way to revival; preacher pouts as Nineveh is saved.

E-mail Channel: The latest letters from Paul to Corinth, Ephesus, Philippi, Thessalonica, and our church. A legitimate way to read someone else's mail.

Adventure Time: Thousands of Hebrews barely escape Egyptian chariots; political rival on the run from deranged king; woman defeats invaders with a tent peg; prostitute hides spies who plot the destruction of a major city.

BSPN: Amazing physical challenges: long-haired man destroys city with his bare hands; teenager kills giant; small band of Hebrews conquer Jericho.

Bible Talk: Dysfunctional families on this week: see brothers who kill, cheat, and sell family members into slavery; royal family shocked when brother rapes sister; "Mother always liked him best," sobs elder brother.

Family Matters: Wayward son returns home; virtuous

woman defined; the harvest season becomes a time of bud-
ding romance for a foreign woman and a rich landowner;
barren widow turns prostitute to assure her dead husband
an heir; man fooled by veil marries wrong woman; wives
vie for supremacy in a race to bear children.

God-solved Mysteries: Man hears burning bush talk;
hungry multitude fed by small boy's lunch; man dead four
days comes to life; boys thrown in furnace emerge un-
harmed; man spends night with lion without a scratch;
blind man receives sight.

Future Network: Elderly disciple sees visions of
things to come; abominable harlots, horrible beasts, the
Bride of Christ, a hero on a white horse. See heaven open;
eat at the marriage supper of the Lamb; experience the end
of time firsthand.

Biography: Life of the Son of God told by eyewitness-
es; actual words recorded; tragedy is turned to victory as
crucified Messiah comes to life.

Of course, the Bible was not made for TV. That was
just a fun way to review the variety found in the Bible.
However, all the above stories—and more—are there.

Many Christians have grouped the various types of
writing found in the Bible into seven categories. The Old
Testament consists of the *law* (first five books of the Bible),
12 books of *history*, 5 books of *wisdom literature*, and 17
books of the *prophets*. The New Testament is made up of 5
history books (four Gospels and the Book of Acts), 21 *Epistles* (or letters), and the *apocalypse* (Revelation).

Other Bible students group the Scriptures according to
the variety of styles found in the Bible. *Literary* types of
writing include narrative and lyric poetry. All other forms
in the Scriptures are *expository* writings. (See the chart at
the end of this chapter for examples.)

Everybody Loves a Story

Can we remember the first stories we heard, perhaps

in that warm spot by a loving parent's side? The closeness, the excitement of seeing what might be on the next page, the security of that familiar voice that made us beg, "Tell me a story."

What do we remember from the sermon last Sunday? Can we recite its three main points from memory? Probably not, as profound as that sermon might have been. But chances are that if the minister told a story—a good story—to illustrate the point, we still remember that.

Perhaps that is why God planned for the majority of the Bible to be in story form. It is His story of the history of His love for His people: the love with which He created us, the tragedy of our rejection of that love, and the outpouring of His grace to re-create us into His people again.

The Word Made Flesh

Good stories are always concrete. They give us things to see, hear, and feel. When John said, "The Word became flesh and made his dwelling among us" (John 1:14), we know he was referring to Christ's incarnation—His coming to earth as a man to live with us. But from the very beginning, God has made His message "flesh" through the stories of His people and His interaction with them. These accounts, too, live with us—real-live stories for real-live people.

Who can forget Cain, the first murderer? As the voice of his brother's blood cries to him from the ground, the voice of his Creator speaks to him as well: "What have you done?" (Genesis 4:10). While Cain is punished for his crime, he is also protected by the grace of God's mark. The elemental picture of grace comes into sharper focus as God's story continues. And from the time of Cain's parents to the end of God's book, we see how sinful people are restored by grace: the Israelites who worshiped idols, the great David who killed his lover's husband, the woman taken in adultery, the fearful follower who denied his master three times. It's the classic struggle of good versus evil—and good wins. He wants us to remember it.

The Greatest Story Ever Told, and Told, and Told, and . . .

When we grab a book off the shelf for some leisure reading, what do we choose? Adventure? Mystery? War stories? Romance? Self-help? Biography? Whatever our tastes, the Bible has something to offer.

It thrills us with adventure like the epic tale of Moses who leads God's people out of bondage and into the land of promise. The story of Esther, the undercover Jewess placed in a pagan palace just at the right time to save her people from another holocaust, intrigues us. Rahab, the prostitute innkeeper with a red scarf, helps the Hebrews conquer Jericho and saves her life as well, gaining her acceptance into the family of God's chosen people. It warms us with the romance of Ruth and the picture of her wise and faithful mother-in-law whose inconsolable grief finally turns to the joy of a new grandson in her arms.

It shares sad tales of love spurned with the story of Jacob's "weak-eyed" wife and the beautiful younger sister whom the husband preferred, or Tamar deserted by her dead husband's family. We cringe as Saul seals his doom with a visit to a witch at Endor and mourn the tragic Absalom hanging from a tree as we hear the plaintive sounds of his father David crying, "O my son Absalom! My son, my son Absalom! If only I had died instead of you—O Absalom, my son, my son!" (2 Samuel 18:33).

We even find tales of inexplicable evil such as the story in Judges of the Levite's concubine who was thrown outside to a gang of men who "abused her throughout the night" (Judges 19:25). The picture of her dead hand reaching for the threshold shows us something about grace by the horrible picture of its absence.

What's in the Future?

Would we like to look into the future? Are we fascinated by visions and dreams? We are when we meet Daniel or see John's revelations. What terrifying pictures! John's vision in Revelation confronts us with the horrors of the enemy: a "red dragon with seven heads" (12:3), a war in heaven between the angels and the dragon, the "pale horse" of death (6:8), beasts from the sea and beasts from the earth, omens of earthquakes and famine in the last days. Image after gruesome image shows us with symbolic power the forces of evil this fallen world has amassed.

What awesome pictures. In the midst of "seven golden lampstands" (1:12) in the glory of that light, shines one

"like a son of man," dressed in a robe reaching down to his feet and with a golden sash round his chest. His head and hair were white like wool, as white as snow, and his eyes were like blazing fire. His feet were like bronze glowing in a furnace, and his voice was like the sound of rushing waters. In his right hand he held seven stars, and out of his mouth came a sharp double-edged sword. His face was like the sun shining in all its brilliance (vv. 13-16).

Taken literally, the picture described here would be frightening and disturbing; but through symbolism John uses the power of literary description to show us the awesome presence of God: His blinding light; the purity of His holiness; the majesty of His power, shining like gold.

Wanted: a Hero

In the classic adventure stories written by the Greeks and Romans, the hero is easy to recognize. He is a man larger than life who could rule a kingdom, plot the demise of the enemy, consort with gods and goddesses, swim for days in the ocean, and win the gold medal at any Olympic contest.

Biblical heroes are quite different.

Give me the name of a great king. Saul? They had to draft him for the job. He hid behind the baggage. Later he became paranoid and deranged. David? He committed adultery, murdered his best soldier to cover his crime, and failed as a father.

Show me a great leader. Moses? All he could do was stutter, "N-n-n-not m-m-m-m-me," when God called him. Gideon? He needed fleeces to test God's message, and his family was known for idol worship.

Name a great woman of the Bible. Rahab? She was a prostitute and a Canaanite—no Jewish blood in her veins. Ruth? Widowed, dependent on the favor of in-laws for survival. Tamar? Widowed twice, childless, she impersonated a prostitute in order to have sons according to the Levitical law.

How about Peter as a hero? When being Christian was no longer politically correct, he three times denied ever knowing Christ.

What happened to these flawed and reluctant heroes?

David became Israel's greatest king, a man after God's own heart.

Gideon defeated Midian with only 300 men.

Rahab helped Joshua's army defeat Jericho and was saved by the spies she helped.

Ruth found love and security in Boaz's arms.

Tamar was acquitted of wrong and bore a double blessing—twins—joining Rahab and Ruth in the genealogy of Christ.

Peter became the rock on which Christ said He would build His church.

Only Saul's story ended in failure, not because he was any less heroic than the rest but because of his lack of faith in God's grace.

Heroes? Certainly not—until God in His grace used such people to do extraordinary things.

Only the Divine Need Apply

So who is *the* hero? God himself. From the very first story we actually see God as a part of the action, walking with and talking to His creation.

The Greeks could never understand this kind of God. To them, the most important characteristic of a god was his apathy, the inability to feel for human beings lest they in some way might control the god's emotions and thus gain power over him. Conversely, the biblical stories show a God who is intimately involved in the lives of His people, a God who comes to live with them and ultimately dies for them. We see that because our God chooses to be the hero in every story.

Food for Our Senses

Stories are not all the Bible has to offer. The cynicism of Solomon in Ecclesiastes, the passionate expressions of love in Song of Songs, the wise sayings of Proverbs, the woeful warnings of many of the prophets, and, of course, the psalms are all in poetic form.

Many people are often afraid of poetry, but nothing else can go so deeply into the spirit or grip the imagination quite like its images. Who has not in a moment of despair turned to one of the psalms of lament? Christ did that on the Cross as He poured out His feelings of abandonment, "My God, my God, why have you forsaken me?" (Psalm 22:1).

Laments comprise more than one-third of the psalms in the Bible, so such moods must be appropriate expressions before God. In fact, one whole book is devoted to lamentations, and the drama of Job contains many lament poems. By the end of each expression, however, the woeful petition turns to statements of confidence: "The poor will eat and be satisfied; they who seek the LORD will praise him" (Psalm 22:26).

These psalms show how a gracious God has ears to hear our cries.

The psalms of praise—both personal and communal—tell of the wonders of God's creation and the many evidences of His faithfulness to His people: "The heavens declare the glory of God" (19:1). Even the heavens "talk" of His goodness. Their images also show us pictures of the godly, like a "tree planted by streams of water, which yields its fruit in season" (1:3).

The love poetry of Solomon communicates the idealized love of the bridegroom for his bride:

"How beautiful you are, my darling!

Oh, how beautiful!

Your eyes behind your veil are doves . . .

All beautiful you are, my darling;

there is no flaw in you" (Song of Songs 4:1, 7).

The admonitions of Proverbs give us vivid pictures of the foolish and the wise. "Like snow in summer or rain in harvest, honor is not fitting for a fool" (26:1). "The tongue of the righteous is choice silver, but the heart of the wicked is of little value" (10:20).

Something for the Left-Brained

Do we enjoy ideas that challenge our thinking? Are self-help books our choice? Do we turn first to the editorial page of our daily newspapers? Then follow the theological arguments of Paul or the clear logic of the writer to the Hebrews. Matthew gives lists of Christ's ethical teachings, and Paul's letters offer clear practical guidelines. This "God-help" material will teach us how to live a godly life.

Ears to Hear

When people discuss a story or try to understand a poem, someone is bound to say, "Why don't they just say what they mean and forget all this symbolism stuff?" That's a good question. If God wanted us to get His message, why wouldn't He just say something we could learn by rote and be done with it?

Unfortunately gaining wisdom is not that easy. The reader who would find wisdom has work to do to make that truth his or her own. Perhaps that is why the Book of Job needs 42 chapters of dramatic dialogue that cycles and recycles to teach us why good people suffer and why suffering in God's world always has meaning. The story is framed at the beginning and the end with a narrative of Job's plight and redemption. But inside that frame are a series of laments and poetic admonitions from his so-called friends—all trying to do the hard work of coming to an understanding of his suffering. Such questions have no easy answers, so we, too, have to journey with Job.

When God finally breaks the cycle by answering Job—again in poetry—out of the whirlwind, He gives no simple explanation for what Job has experienced. Instead, through vivid images, He shows Job the wonders of His creative power with a catalog of His creative acts: "Where were you when I laid the earth's foundation?" (38:4). The answer is as complex as the infinite works of an awesome God.

It is only then that Job comes to terms with his suffering. Not when all his wealth is restored as we materialists might like to think but when he "sees" God. The seeing, though, took painful work on his part.

In a similar way, the many literary forms of the Scriptures call us to do difficult and sometimes painful work if we, too, would mine its treasures.

When Jesus wanted to teach His disciples what the word "neighbor" meant, He didn't give a simple dictionary definition. He told a story of a poor man mugged on the highway, passed over by the spiritual leaders of the day who were too busy trying to get to their board meetings on time. Then He showed a Samaritan who took time to help and heal. And then they knew what a "neighbor" was. A memorized definition would have been forgotten in time; how many of us, though, can ever forget the compelling plot or vivid images of this story? The definition of "neighbor" is now a part of us. (See Luke 10:30-37.)

After many of His parables, Jesus makes a puzzling statement, "He who has ears, let him hear" (Matthew 11:15; 13:9; 13:43; see Mark 4:9; Luke 8:8; 14:35). If we do the work of trying to understand the meaning of the story, we will "hear" the message. It will become ours.

One Story, One Plot

Ultimately the multitude of experiences and forms of the Bible tell one beautiful story—the story of a God who became our Hero, our Friend who died for us so that we could live again, who always was and always will be the Creator of life and the Mediator of grace.

The story that reveals God to us began with the creation of heaven and earth, and it ends that way too. In the last chapters of the last book, Revelation, a world is created again, "a new heaven and a new earth" (21:1). "There will be no more night. They will not need the light of a lamp or the light of the sun, for the Lord God will give them light. And they will reign for ever and ever" (22:5).

Heaven has opened. The Bridegroom has come on a white horse to claim His bride. The Marriage Supper is served, "the great supper of God" (19:17). Death and all hell are thrown into the lake of fire. Eden is restored, ever more glorious and now eternal. The good guys have won. What an ending!

On every page from beginning to end we have the good news, the gospel, so good it must be told again and again in every possible form.

Background Scripture: Genesis 4:10; Judges 19:25; 2 Samuel 18:33; Job 38:1; Psalms 1:3; 19:1; 22:1, 26; Proverbs 10:20, 26; Song of Songs 5:1; Matthew 11:15; 13:9, 43; Mark 4:9; Luke 8:8, 10:30-37; 14:35; John 1:14; Revelation 1:12-16; 6:8; 12:3; 19:17; 21:1; 22:5

Memory Verse: Psalm 119:11

Types of Writing in Scripture*
Literary
Narrative
    Epic—Exodus
    Gospel—Matthew; Mark; Luke; John
    Heroic Narrative—Genesis 11—50
    Miracles—Mark 9:14-29
    Oratory—2 Chronicles 6:12-42; Matthew 5—7
    Parables—Luke 16:1-13; Matthew 20:1-16
    Romance—Esther; Ruth
    Resurrection Appearances—Luke 24:13-49
    Satire—Jonah; Judges 3:12-30; Luke 18:9-14; Matthew
       23
    Story of Origins (Primordial History)—Genesis 3:1-24
    Tragedy—1 Samuel (Story of Saul); Judges 13—16
    Visionary (Apocalyptic Writing)—Revelation
Lyric Poetry
    Acrostic Psalms—Psalms 9; 34
    Communal (Liturgical) Psalms—Psalms 74; 137; 136
    Epithalamion (Wedding Poetry)—Song of Songs 2:3-7
    Lament—Psalms 22; 54; Lamentations
    Ode—Psalm 139
    Parody—Psalm 29
    Pastoral—Song of Songs 1:7-8
    Praise—Psalms 18; 19; 96
    Prophecy—Isaiah 40
    Songs of Zion (Songs of Ascent)—Psalms 27; 121
    Wisdom Literature—Ecclesiastes
    Proverbs
    Drama—Job
Expository
    History—Joshua 8:1-29
    Ethical Teachings—Matthew 5:17-48
    Legal Writing—Leviticus 19; Exodus 20

Letters (Epistles)
    Theological Argument—Romans 6—8
    Practical Guidelines—1 Corinthians 14
    Theological Exposition—Hebrews

Dr. Peggy Poteet is a professor of English at Southern Nazarene University, Bethany, Oklahoma.

*Suggested by Leland Ryken and Jirair Tashjian

8

What It Means to Me

by Walt Russell

THE WEEKLY BIBLE STUDY BEGAN with comfortable predictability. After the customary pie, the members got cups of coffee and settled into their familiar niches around the room. Charlie, the leader, cleared his throat to signal that things were starting. As he did with merciless regularity each week, he began with the question, "Well, what do these verses mean to you?"

The discussion followed a familiar pattern. Each responded to what the verses meant to him or her, and the group reached its weekly general consensus—at least on the easier verses. They all knew what was coming, however: another stalemate between Donnell and Maria. Donnell had been a Christian for several years and was the self-appointed, resident theologian. For some reason he always seemed to lock horns with Maria, a relatively new Christian, yet an enthusiastic student of the Bible.

The scene repeated itself every time they came to difficult verses. The passages would elicit conflicting interpretations. Donnell would contend vehemently for the interpretation of his former pastor, which usually seemed a bit forced to the rest of the group. But it was Maria, being new and perhaps more straightforward, who would challenge Donnell. Because she didn't know the Bible that well yet, she would relate the difficult verse to her Christian experience in a way that contradicted Donnell's interpretation. Donnell would only redouble his efforts.

The stalemate usually ended with Charlie, the leader, or Betty, the resident peacemaker, bringing "resolution" to the discussion. One of them would calmly conclude by saying, "Well, this is another example of how reading the Bible is a matter of personal interpretation and how a verse can mean one thing to one person and something else to another." The group members would leave with a vague, hollow feeling in their chests.

A recent Barna Research Group survey on what Americans believe confirms what this brief scenario illustrates: We are in danger of becoming a nation of relativists. The Barna survey asked, "Is there absolute truth?" Amazingly 66 percent of American adults responded that they believe "there is no such thing as absolute truth; different people can define truth in conflicting ways and still be correct." The figure rises to 72 percent when it comes to those between the ages of 18 and 25.

Before we stoop to cast the first stones, we Evangelicals might ask if we are without sin in this matter, especially when it comes to our approach to interpreting the Bible. I believe we may unwittingly contribute to the widespread malaise of relativistic thinking. Indeed, our big educational standbys—Sunday School, the adult Bible study, and the sermon—may help spread the disease.

A Mouthful of Confusing Signals

"What does this verse mean to you?" It is stunning how often we use this cliché to signal the beginning of the interpretive time in Bible studies and Sunday School classes. But the question may send a mouthful of confusing signals.

First, it confuses the *meaning* of a passage with the *significance* of the passage. Meaning is what the author intended the passage to say. Significance, on the other hand, is a relationship between that meaning and a person or situation.*

The *meaning* of a text never changes. Our first goal is to discover this fixed thing. In contrast, the *significance* of that text to me and to others is very fluid and flexible.

By confusing these two aspects of the interpretation process, we Evangelicals approach the Bible with an interpretive relativism. If it means one thing to you and something contradictory to me, we have no ultimate court of appeals. We can never establish and validate "the one correct interpretation." In fact, our language and approach suggest that there is no such animal.

In conservative Christian circles this has tragically led to people seeing the authority of God residing in the most powerful preachers of His Word rather than in the Word itself. This explains Donnell's appeal, "But *my pastor says* . . ."

Second, the question, "What does this verse mean to you?" reflects a drift in determining meaning that has been going on for a century in literary circles. The classical approach was to focus on *the authors* and their historical and (later) emotional setting in life. Earlier in the 20th century the focus shifted to *the text*, and authors lost their special rights to explain what their text means. Texts allegedly take on a life of their own apart from their authors.

However, the drift has not stopped at the text. The focus for determining meaning is now on *the interpreter*. The reader allegedly "creates meaning."

Applied to biblical study, interpretation shifts from discovering the absolute truths of God's Word to winning others over to what the text "means to *us* because our system for explaining it is the most internally coherent and satisfying." The best we can hope for is to persuade others

---

*This point has been made by literary critic E. D. Hirsch Jr. in his book *Validity in Interpretation*. Hirsch asserts that *"meaning* is that which is represented by a text; it is what the author meant. . . . *Significance,* on the other hand, names a relationship between that meaning and a person, or a conception, or a situation, or indeed anything imaginable."

to join our interpretive community, at least until a more coherent and satisfying interpretation comes along.

Avoiding Relativism

What can we do to avoid this relativism?

First, we need to clean up our language when we talk about Scripture. If we want to discuss the *meaning* of the text, then we ask, "What does this verse or text mean?" If we want to discuss *significance*, then ask, "What is the relevance or significance of this verse to you?"

Second, we must differentiate between *our emotional posture* (tolerant and sensitive) and *our view of the truth* (something absolute, which can be determined). We show sensitivity but avoid giving up too much "real estate." Establishing correct meanings sometimes entails lots of interpretive work. When disagreements arise, it is tempting to retreat from the hard work under the banner of tolerance and sensitivity. Instead, we should underscore in a loving, sensitive manner that only one of several conflicting interpretations can be correct. This correct interpretation can be validated as the most likely one primarily by following the main theme of the passage's immediate context.

As Bible students, we prefer to head for immediate application. We are therefore constantly tempted to skip the hard work of determining a biblical text's meaning and move quickly to the text's personal relevance. Such exploration will take time, and it may be challenging. The historical or literary context seldom "sizzles." The challenge is to see the setting of other people's lives and questions as interesting as our own.

Many of us are unwilling to establish the passage's literary context by tracing the biblical book's logical development. Or we do not establish the historical context by reading background material in a Bible dictionary, a Bible encyclopedia, or a good commentary.

Why? Increasingly we do not see value in establishing

a passage's historical and literary context. In believing that God's Word directly addresses us, we ignore that He speaks to our needs *through* the historical and literary contexts of the people of the Bible.

But the reward for such work is that we have the controls and safeguard of the original context that the Holy Spirit used when He inspired the passage. The absence of such work increases our chances of emerging with wrong meaning, wrong emphasis, and wrong application. It may even negate the Holy Spirit's power in our application of that passage.

Focusing on the felt needs makes it easy to end up with a great need desperately in search of a passage. The current emphasis on shorter topical preaching and topical Bible studies may unwittingly help feed this relativism in application. The mistake is a fundamental one: elevating the hearers' context over the Bible's. Instead of holding the Bible's context and our contemporary context in a dynamic tension, we assume that the contemporary context is the most important one.

This perspective may be more dangerous than we think. It assumes a human-centered worldview. Therefore, the burden is upon each individual to wring some sense out of life through the exercise of personal choice. If we unwittingly cater to this worldview, God and His Word become reduced to helpful items on life's smorgasbord of options that bring fulfillment.

It would be far better to appeal to a genuine felt need and then challenge the worldview that surrounds that need. Our culture's context—a human-centered worldview living only in the present moment—needs to be confronted by the Bible's context—a historical and God-centered worldview. Verses isolated from their literary contexts seldom achieve such a confrontation. Whole paragraphs discussed within the flow of broader sections come much closer.

Our Needs Are Not Enough

An example of how this works can be illustrated by an approach to a four-part Bible series in the light of today's strong felt need for happiness.

We might remember that Paul's letter to the Philippians was about "joy" and "rejoicing." A quick read confirms the presence of those words. We have already determined our general *targeted need* in this series (people's hunger for happiness), and we have already assumed our general *conclusion* for the series (God wants to meet our need for happiness). Therefore, what we are really looking for are interesting and specific biblical bridges from our targeted need to our conclusion. So far, so good. But here is where the weeds get taller and the briers sharper.

We first face a choice about how much time and energy we are going to spend on uncovering the historical, cultural, and literary backgrounds of the Epistle to the Philippians. It seems straightforward enough: True happiness and joy come from knowing Christ and thereby being able to rejoice in any circumstance. A four-part Bible study series might look like this:

- Joy in friendship (1:3-5)
- Joy in perseverance (1:25-26)
- Joy in teamwork (2:1-4)
- Joy in God's peace (with a low-key evangelistic emphasis) (4:4-7)

Here we have an expository series with some continuity from one book of the Bible. We address significant emotional needs of both non-Christians and Christians within our culture. And we address some of the key issues people face. Nearly every group in the church should find something in this approach to satisfy them.

But instead of doing the hard work of investigating the Epistle's historical and literary context, we make the mistake of assuming *our* context is the main context that matters. We thereby distort the meaning of these four passages.

The perspective of our existence, for example, sets up happiness or joy as the goal. We also distort Paul's understanding of the gospel in Philippians if we interpret this Epistle from our fulfillment perspective. If personal joy and peace are our primary concerns, the gospel is reduced to the God-given means for achieving this kind of fulfillment. It becomes a modern fix-all.

The biblical perspective sees joy as a by-product of involvement in the gospel cause. By interpreting Paul's eight uses of the word "gospel" in Philippians within their original literary and historical context, we see that the gospel was something in which the Philippians shared in partnership (1:5) and in which Euodia and Syntyche shared Paul's struggle (4:2-3). The gospel was something Paul defended and confirmed (1:7) and that supplied the standard for the Philippians' conduct as they strove for the faith of it (v. 27). Ironically, Paul's present sufferings turned out for the greater progress of the gospel (v. 12), and Timothy's serving of Paul helped further the gospel (2:22).

The gospel, then, is not something that exists solely for *our* progress and personal fulfillment (although it does include these things). Rather, the gospel is something to which we are to give ourselves for *its* progress and fulfillment. The gospel is God's program for worldwide salvation.

When we go to the text first, we come to what Paul means by "joy." The scriptural definition of "joy" controls our Bible study, rather than starting from our felt need for happiness, an idea not addressed in this passage. When we give ourselves to the spreading of the gospel, we will endure hardship. In the difficulties, we will also experience the joy Paul was describing.

Only by entering into the cultural, historical, and literary context of Philippians will we grasp this insight. Significant temporal, cultural, and language gaps will need to be bridged. But isn't this why God has given the church Spirit-gifted teachers who can take advantage of the wealth of Bible study tools and helps?

Conclusion

A brief visit to a good Christian bookstore will quickly reinforce the fact that no other people in the history of the Church have been blessed with our dizzying array of Bible study aids. Our downfall is not a lack of resources but a lack of understanding about their necessity.

We must establish the original historical and literary context of biblical passages. Once this work is done, *then* we can move to determining the needs a passage addresses. But the *text,* not our concerns, initially determines the focus. To ignore the necessity of this task is to risk sliding into relativism. We find few contextual safeguards in this land of "what it means to me" and probably very little of God's voice.

Background Scripture: Philippians 1:3-27; 2:1-4, 22; 4:2-7

Memory Verse: 2 Timothy 2:15

Dr. Walt Russell teaches New Testament at Biola University in La Mirada, California.

This article first appeared in the October 26, 1992, issue of *Christianity Today.* Reprinted with the author's permission.

9

Navigating New Territory

by Joseph Seaborn

THE BIBLE IS THE TRUTH OF GOD gathered into a community of truths. Between Genesis 1 and Revelation 22, there are 1,189 chapters crowded with lofty and life-related truths. When we read the Bible, we are privileged, as the French thinker Blaise Pascal put it, "to think God's thoughts after Him."

In many ways, unlocking our understanding of the Bible is a lot like getting to know a new community. We don't just drive into a new city or town and have a feel for it overnight. It takes time, energy, alertness, and a willingness to change earlier impressions.

When we approach the community of truths in the Bible, we need similar patience and commitment. But it's a venture worth eternity. The friendships we cultivate, the experiences we share, and the insights we gain enrich our lives now and give us a hint of heaven to come.

For each of the stages of insight through which we pass on our way to unlocking the deeper truths of God, there are dangers and benefits. At the end of each section I have noted at least one of each. Take a moment to reflect on them.

Introducing Ourselves to the Community

Most of us have had the experience of moving into a new community. During those first few days, we can't take the shortcuts because we don't know them. We drive all over the map to get to a place only four or five blocks away. If our cars need repair, we open the yellow pages and pray they will treat us fairly. We have to ask around at the church we are visiting to find out who is the best doctor.

Those early days in a new community can be frustrating. One-way roads—going the wrong way. Stop signs cropping up just over the tops of hills. Lanes that merge and crowd us off the road. "Locals" looking at us funny because we are lost—and look it. Early on, the learning curve is high.

For people who are just beginning their walk with Christ, the awkwardness and frustration can be equally high. If we didn't grow up in a Bible-based home, we remember well how clumsy we felt trying to find Matthew and thinking that somebody was mispronouncing the Book of Job!

For the first time in the history of Western culture, more than 50 percent of high schoolers have neither a parent nor a grandparent who is Christian. In one poll conducted on a Christian college campus, more than 55 percent of the freshmen could not name the four Gospels, and more than 60 percent could not name one of the major prophets, let alone a minor one. If we sometimes feel we are biblically illiterate, take heart. We are not alone.

Sitting in any given church on a Sunday morning are those who still need to turn to the table of contents to find a book of the Bible, another group who know enough to rummage around in the general area, still others who can turn right to it, and a few who can quote it ahead of the pastor.

No matter what our age and stage of biblical knowledge, there are plenty of ways for gaining a greater understanding of God's eternal Word. From the *American Stan-*

dard Version, which translates from the original Hebrew (Old Testament) and Greek (New Testament) in a very literal way, to *The Message,* which takes considerable liberty with the original terms, there are numerous translations and paraphrases that try to bring us close to what the Bible authors were trying to say.

Just as there are plenty of sources for getting better acquainted with a new community, so there are plenty of tools for getting to know more about the Bible.

When we move into a new community, we turn to agencies such as the Chamber of Commerce or the mayor's office. We scour the yellow pages for basic services. We chat with neighbors across the street.

When trying to unlock the truths of the Bible, there are several sources that help us get our bearings. *Concordances* help us track down a passage based on a key word. Most concordances are alphabetically arranged so that we can look up the word "grace" under the Gs and find every biblical occurrence laid out in one column.

Bible dictionaries gather up the main persons, places, and themes of the Bible and offer an explanatory article for each one. The article usually concludes with a list of related topics that appear elsewhere in the same dictionary. An article on the "Wise Men," for example, might close by saying, "See also 'Magi,' 'Nativity,' and 'Herod.'"

Several other specialized sources help unlock the eternal truths of the Bible. *Bible atlases* focus on the landscape of the Bible world, providing maps, 3-D drawings, and illustrations to help us visualize a particular event or journey in Bible times. Atlases allow us to picture David's battle strategy, understand better why there was so much friction between the Samaritans and the Jews, or see why the "land bridge" of Israel was overrun by so many powerful empires during its colorful history.

Commentaries help us by giving the background, key terms, and general meaning of a biblical passage. Commentaries come in every length and quality, ranging in emphasis from devotional to exegetical (which get into the technical features of a particular passage). Commentaries reflect the theological slant of their authors, so we need to be aware that a commentary should not be taken on the same plane of authority as the Bible itself. Only the Bible remains the authoritative Word of God.

On average, we will find that commentaries are richer with insight and nearer to the original meaning if the author has become a specialist on one book or a small group of books such as the Gospel of John and the three letters of John. We can find sets of commentaries on the entire 66 books of the Bible written by one author. However that usually means that the commentaries lack depth simply because one person cannot be that knowledgeable and space is too limited to be detailed.

Various translations, when read in comparison, can also greatly add to our understanding of a passage. One version of the Bible will translate the word *doulos* as "slave" while another will use the word "servant." Frankly, the word "slave" is a little closer to the original mood of the word, but we can see how reading both translations will give us a better sense of this one term.

Translations are trying to achieve what they call "dynamic equivalency." That is, they are trying to find words in one language to repeat the idea communicated in the original language. One Greek term, for example, may have five or six English words that would almost say it—but not quite. That's why it's wise to look at several translations to come closer to an accurate understanding of the idea.

All of these sources and more are available on computer software, including brilliant, full-color maps that rival anything found in the backs of our Bibles.

Perhaps we've also noticed that in those early days in a new community we can hardly enjoy the local scenery for watching the road signs. We can't yet drive by habit, so we have to consciously select every road and check the signs at every turn.

Early exploration of the Bible can be equally awkward. I remember a student who came up one day after a New Testament class, "Hey, Prof, this is really good stuff, but I'm lost. I had no idea Jesus had 12 . . . what did you call those men?"

"Disciples," I told him.

"Disciples," he repeated. He took two steps and turned back around, "Prof, do you think Jesus would let me be a disciple?"

Prior to coming to college, that young man had been to church only three times in his life. For him, terms like "the Exodus," "salvation," and "Isle of Patmos" might as well have been in Latin. But he was committed to getting them down. Nearly every step he took required a commentary, an atlas, or a dictionary, but he stuck to it. Today he is on the evangelism team in his church, sharing that same Word with a great deal more confidence as he knocks on doors and invites people to Jesus.

Greatest Danger: *Being so overwhelmed with the incredible amount there is to know that we throw in the towel and give up.*

Greatest Benefit: *Enjoying the sheer delight of learning so much about the Bible in a short time. We feel like a canary trying to get a drink at a fire hydrant!*

Learning Our Way Around

After a few visits to a community, we begin to know our way around. We wean ourselves from all the road signs and begin to observe the character and details of the community: the homes, the business districts, the industrial parks, the green parks.

It doesn't take long to realize that within the larger community we have several smaller communities. Areas of a community are zoned as "residential," "industrial," or "enterprise."

The more we get into the Word, the more we realize that it contains several types of literature, each of which requires a slightly different approach if we want to understand it clearly. If we read the psalms of David, we can't help but feel the emotion spilling over the edge of his soul. Not so in the Ten Commandments of Exodus 20. They are clear-cut commands straight from the mind of God telling us what to do and what not to do in order to live a holy life. From there we can page over to Revelation and run across mysterious symbols that often leave even the best students of Scripture scratching their heads.

When getting to know a new community, we want to explore it in its natural divisions. We would never go into a community and say that just because a doghouse, a fire station, and a stop sign are all red that somehow the residents intend for us to link them together in the same thought. The fact that all three are red is only incidental. We shouldn't make much of it. Likewise, when we turn to the Bible, we want to avoid picking out a single term from several passages and assuming that we understand it well just because we have several examples of its usage. That is just as unnatural to Bible study as it would be in surveying a new community.

When exploring the Bible, we must remember that each unit or section of Scripture has one main meaning but many applications. Just as a stop sign means only one thing (other options are possible, but have the checkbook handy!), so we should assume that paragraphs of the Bible have one main meaning. Our first question of a Bible passage should never be, "How does this passage strike me?" but rather, "What did the author mean to say?" Once we know what he meant to say, then we can apply it to our lives today. Failing to let the author speak first is like intentionally running a stop sign. We act as if we know better than the author what he was trying to say, and we can interpret the truths of the Bible in any old way that strikes our fancy.

Most students of culture will tell us that the best way to get to know a community is to become familiar with the family units. Families come in all shapes and sizes. Scripture, too, is best understood if we look at a "family" of ideas that sit together in a single passage. Before we link the passage with other scripture—in a process called "cross-referencing"—we want to first see how that family of ideas blends together on its own. What are the key ideas in that unit of thought? What was the author trying to say by including that paragraph or chapter? What truths would we lose if that section were missing from the Bible?

In order to gain the greatest insight into a community, we also need to keep moving around among the whole community. If we spend all our time at the post office or with eight-year-olds in a second grade classroom, we will miss the ball games and the parades, the mayhem at the mall, and the fresh air of the wide-open spaces.

In reading the Bible, we need to keep working back and forth among the 66 books and the 40 authors. If we linger too long in the Old Testament, we miss meeting Jesus in person. If we fixate on Acts, we may soar in our knowledge of Early Church history but miss out on the deeper reflection Peter and Paul bring to the gospel message in the books that follow.

Many people fail to find the balance, which a study of the whole Bible brings, and trail off into heresy. They forget that the Bible is a community of truths intended to be seen in harmony and balance. They grab a single idea and run off, assuming they have captured the whole. Just as we only begin to understand persons when we see them within the context of their family, their neighborhood, and finally the whole community, so we must let the truths of the Bible come to us in the same way. A truth needs to be seen in its immediate context or paragraph, then within its book setting, and finally against the backdrop of the entire Bible.

It is best if we can use a translation of the Bible that is formatted in paragraph form. Translations that divide up the whole Bible into individual verses without any paragraph markings fool us into thinking that once we have read a verse, we have the writer's complete idea.

If we have moved into a community, we also know that members of that community often have a number of expressions that only they understand. We can be thoroughly confused until someone blurts out, "It's just the way we say things around here." For instance, I have heard people say, "Take and carry this package to the post office . . ." or "Let's take and go to the store . . ." Everything they do is "Take and . . ."

The Bible does a similar thing. When Jesus shares a profound statement, He prefaces it with the words "Verily, verily" or "truly, truly." Just the expression "Jesus said . . ." would be enough. But that's just the way they said things in Bible times. If we don't have an "insider's" knowledge, we might think that when Jesus said to hate your father and mother He was being harsh (see Luke 14:26). When we realize that He meant to be more loyal to God than even your closest relative, it makes good sense.

Greatest Danger: *Getting to know the Bible but only in a very limited and scattered sense. Being content with knowing only a small part of the full spectrum of biblical truth.*

Greatest Benefit: *Discovering that the Bible is a far-ranging book, covering every dimension of human life and need.*

Taking Up Residence

No matter how loudly people may argue about their love and loyalty to a community, their words won't mean much until they actually move in. They can claim it's the most wonderful community in the world, one in which they want to spend the rest of their lives; but until they "pull up stakes" and move into that community, we won't believe them.

Perhaps we've met people who treat God and the Bible the same way. They can spin out a hundred stories they heard in Sunday School and argue that the Bible is the greatest book in all the world. But until they actually accept the Savior who stands behind the Book, they are still just mouthing words.

Many critics ridicule the Bible as a book crammed with contradictions. They say, for instance, that Paul taught that we are saved by faith while James argued that it happens by works. But their cynicism blinds them from seeing that Paul's audience needed one emphasis in order to strike a balance, while James's readers needed another. Just because an English teacher makes a note on a paper, "watch spelling errors," and never mentions grammar or punctuation does not mean that she doesn't care about subjects and question marks. It simply means that in this paper the spelling is poor.

As a resident of a community, we also need to keep interacting with various age-groups. There are nursing homes, but there are also kindergartens. If we would celebrate the whole community, we need to spend time with people of every age. Many people discount the Old Testament as out of date, nothing but ancient customs with no connection to modern life. But we must never forget that people in Old Testament times needed to be saved by faith just as surely as people in New Testament times. Just because the older generation has a few worship practices that don't exactly light our fire does not mean that their faith is inferior. The Bible is one book, not two. In the words of Augustine, the fourth-century Christian writer: "The New [Testament] is in the Old [Testament] contained, the Old is in the New explained."[1]

Again if we visited a community and came upon a jail and knew nothing about why it was there, we could easily assume that the other citizens who placed the people in there were mean and vindictive. But once we understood the purpose of the jail, we would not only see, but agree, that certain people should be locked away for good. Far too many people glance at the Bible and say that just because God destroyed a group of people or just because He asked Abraham to sacrifice his son, He is a vicious God who is out for blood. But if only they would "take up residence" and come to see what God was doing to balance the scales of love and justice, they would realize that the greatest characteristic of the God of the Bible is not anger but holy love.

What D. L. Moody once said of 1 Corinthians 13 ought to be said of the entire Bible, "Many people occasionally take a stroll into 1 Corinthians 13, but very few settle down there."[2]

If beauty lies in the eyes of the beholder, deep biblical insight lies in the heart of the believer. The best way to discover the eternal truths of the Bible is to have eternal life in our hearts, eternal life that comes through personally knowing Jesus Christ by faith. The Bible points to Him, talks about Him, exists for Him. It is a cluster of truths that point to Christ as the supreme Truth. We open our hearts to the Bible best when we have placed our faith in Jesus first. Faith in the Christ of the Bible leads to a greater ability to know the truths of the Bible. When we know Christ personally, we understand why these truths were put there in the first place. As Paul says, "The man without the Spirit does not accept the things that come from the Spirit of God, for they are foolishness to him, and he cannot understand them, because they are spiritually discerned" (1 Corinthians 2:14).

Greatest Danger: *Assuming that knowing a lot about the Bible automatically makes us closer to the God of the Bible. No matter how mature we are, we are only saved by our nearness to Christ rather than by the amount of our knowledge.*

Greatest Benefit: *As we allow the God of the Bible to fill us with His Holy Spirit, we have an increasing yearning to spend time in the Word because we have a growing desire to know more and more about Christ (see 1 Corinthians 2:16).*

Thinking like a Citizen

Most of us have had the experience. We have lived in the community for a while; we know the shortcuts and the back roads. But then the shock. We drive an entire stretch of road and can't remember the actual trip! Our minds were somewhere else, and how we got home safely is a miracle.

It is also possible to reach this stage in our Bible reading. There are people who are so familiar with the Bible that they can quote large sections of it at will. Get them started and they can finish the Christmas story or the 23rd psalm or the various pieces of the Christian armor listed in Ephesians 6.

The danger for those this familiar with the Bible is that they know it so well, they lose the ability to see it with fresh eyes and an open spirit. We sometimes laugh about a familiar stretch of road and say, "I could drive it with my eyes closed." That can happen in our Bible study too.

On the other hand, when we have steeped our minds in the Word of God over many years, we reach a stage when we begin seeing the astounding interconnectedness of the Bible. Instead of thinking in passages, we think in terms of the grand themes, the sweeping patterns, the unity of the whole. Great themes like the kingdom of God or holiness leap out at us in places where we would not have seen them before. The more we mature at this level of insight, the more we come to realize that the Bible is not finally about a thousand things but rather about a handful of eternal things.

Greatest Danger: *The risk of being so familiar with the stories and teachings of Scripture that we no longer need to think about them to recite them. They become to us "rote that we quote without note."*

Greatest Benefit: *The joy of seeing amazing connections in the Bible and the sheer joy of embracing truth we have known forever, but seeing it again for the very first time.*

Conclusion

I like what happened to one scientist. He planned to spend his summer exploring the whole world of nature. At the end of the summer he wrote in his diary, "I spent the whole summer exploring the world of nature. I got halfway across my backyard!" The Bible is equally packed with insight. Those who have eyes to see can spend all summer and only make it halfway across a single book.

Let me make a challenge. Take this theme of "getting to know a community" and think of other ways in which getting to know a new community is a lot like getting to know the community of truths in the Bible. Take the time to jot down the comparisons. It will help us unlock more and more of the great truths of the Bible.

It only takes a moment to save our souls, but it takes a lifetime to save our minds. As we spend time exploring the truths of the Bible, we are saving our minds. John 17:17 parks this truth in the driveway, "Sanctify them by the truth; your word is truth."

Background Scripture: Luke 14:26; John 17:17; 1 Corinthians 2:14, 16

Memory Verse: Romans 15:4

Dr. Joseph Seaborn is a professor and chair of the division of religion and philosophy at Indiana Wesleyan University, Marion, Indiana.

1. James W. Elliott, *The World's Most Amazing Book* (Butler, Ind.: Higley Press, 1959), 119.
2. Dwight L. Moody, *Holding the Fort* (Cincinnati: W. S. Forshee and Co., 1877), 290.

10

Does a Wesleyan Read the Bible Differently?

by Jay Hunton

I LIKE THE STORY ABOUT THE LITTLE BOY who had bought his grandmother a book for her birthday and wanted to write a suitable inscription on the flyleaf. He racked his brain. Suddenly he remembered that his father had a book with an inscription of which he was very proud, so he decided to use it. I can imagine Grandma's surprise when she opened her book, a Bible, and found the following phrase neatly inscribed: "To Grandma, with compliments of the author."

How familiar are we with the Bible? Do we consistently read it? Do we study it? It has many long passages that seem boring. Why should we study the Bible if we find it difficult and, for some, boring?

Why Study the Bible?

The most important reason is that God gave us the Scriptures to provide us with illumination and instruction we need not only to live here on earth but also to inherit eternal life through Jesus Christ, our Savior.

On the road to Emmaus, Jesus clearly explained to two disciples the necessity of Scripture. "He said to them, 'How foolish you are, and how slow of heart to believe all that the prophets have spoken! Did not the Christ have to suffer these things and then enter his glory?' And beginning with Moses and all the Prophets, he explained to them what was said in all the Scriptures concerning himself" (Luke 24:25-27).

Jesus helped them understand His Word. Their response later on speaks of His holy presence: "Were not our hearts burning within us while he talked with us on the road and opened the Scriptures to us?" (Luke 4:32).

Today, the Holy Spirit comes to open the Scripture to us. When we study the Scriptures, He is indispensable to the process, for He will explain and inspire as Jesus did for the two on the road to Emmaus.

Another reason to study the Bible is that it is the supreme authority in matters of faith and conduct. Matthew says, "'Why do your disciples break the tradition of the elders? They don't wash their hands before they eat!' Jesus replied, 'And why do you break the command of God for the sake of tradition? . . . Thus you nullify the Word of God for the sake of tradition'" (15:2-3, 6). The authority of the Word compels us to study the Scriptures so that we might clearly identify the guiding principles for life in Christ.

The Church is a living organism, always adapting to changing circumstances. Various "movements" propel the Church as she tries to reach out in the name of Christ. For example, one author has identified four such movements impacting the Church right now. They are:

- *Personal Evangelism*—stressing the fulfillment of the Great Commission but often neglecting the existing Church
- *Church Renewal*—stressing the Church's fellowship and community life but often neglecting the doctrinal truth
- *Church Growth*—stressing the necessity of numerical growth in churches but often becoming merely a "spiritual technology"

- the *Charismatic Movement* — stressing spiritual gifts and the Holy Spirit's ministry in the Church but often weak in solid biblical teaching[1]

Each of these movements is clearly a key issue in the Church. A steadfast understanding and application of the Word of God must undergird each issue to avoid imbalance and excess. These are important reasons for the necessity in the Church today to read and to study the Bible.

John Wesley's View of Scripture

As a pastor, I have found it gratifying that many of the people in the church want to study the Bible. However, they are often confused when I tell them the traditions and doctrine of the church are Wesleyan. With the variety of approaches to Bible study available, it is important for those in Holiness denominations to begin to understand what is a Wesleyan perspective in reading and studying the Bible.

John Wesley believed that Bible study should include "bringing . . . our experiences of life under grace to Scripture for investigation. The witness of the Holy Spirit testifying to the truth of the passage and applying the truth to the believer's life is absolutely necessary if the Bible is to be illuminated and illuminating."[2] Hence, "Scripture is to be reflected upon in faith through the internal witness of the Holy Spirit."[3] The reader of the Bible must approach the Word in serious and earnest prayer, in self-examination, and in meditation. For Wesley, Scripture and worship are not to be separated. Scripture gains its fullest meaning in worship, public or private.

When Wesleyans understand this approach to reading the Bible, the Scriptures "come alive." They not only describe what they are experiencing under grace but also prescribe what to do about it.

Wesley emphasized the *authority* of the Bible. He commented that he followed the Bible in everything, whether a large or small matter. He did not, however, confine his reading to one book. He was interested in many books, ancient and contemporary. He even encouraged his preachers to read other books as well as the Bible. Yet, when he was considering the final authority of belief and practice, the Bible stood alone because it showed him how to live on earth and how to get to heaven. John Wesley said that theological ideas not supported by Scripture "weigh nothing with me. I allow no other rule, whether of faith or practice, than the Holy Scripture."[4] It was in this sense that he called himself a man of one book.

Wesley strongly believed it was essential that the Bible be *correctly interpreted*. His principle of scriptural interpretation was *interpret Scripture by Scripture*. When some scripture seemed obscure, he encouraged clarifying the passage by those scriptures that speak more plainly.

In this matter of interpretation, Wesley emphasized, also, the importance of *reason*. He felt Paul was one of the great reasoners of Scripture. Wesley wanted to make sure Christians interpreted Scripture correctly, so he produced guidelines for them. He felt that in their reasoning these guidelines would spare his followers from narrow approaches to the Bible.

Wesley thought of the Bible as the guide to *practical religion*. It was often experiences that took Wesley to Scripture, either his own experience or that of others.[5] Experience has vital significance in our practical use of God's Word.

Tradition was essential in the faith of Wesley. For him, tradition included classical writings of the Early Church fathers as well as all the customs of public worship. Hence, Wesley approached the study of Scripture as an act of worship and that involved tradition in some manner—often the same prayers and hymns used in weekly worship services.

It may be helpful to say something about Wesley's *devotional use* of Scripture. He believed the Bible had not been fully encountered until it had been conscientiously applied. He never isolated his use of Scripture from his life of prayer, his reading of other devotional material, or his use of the other means of grace. He used scripture cards that contained a text on one side and a verse from a hymn on the other.[6]

Do Wesleyans Read the Bible Differently?

I believe they do! Let me share some historical Wesleyan guidelines in our approach to the Bible.

Illumination. Let us begin with the illumination of the Holy Spirit through faith. Commenting on 2 Timothy 3:16, "All Scripture is God-breathed and is useful for teaching, rebuking, correcting and training in righteousness," Wesley writes: "The Spirit of God not only once inspired those who wrote [the Scriptures], but continually inspires, [that is] supernaturally assists those that read it with earnest prayer."[7] He believed we need the same Spirit inspiring us to read and understand the Bible that enabled holy men of old to write it. The point is, through the Holy Spirit we are given the faith that illumines the Bible.

Scripture in the Light of Scripture. Wesley urged that the Bible is to be understood in the light of its own identity and direction.[8] We must not use our own ideas for the authority of the Bible. As Isaiah expresses it: "'For my thoughts are not your thoughts, neither are your ways my ways,' declares the LORD" (55:8). Let the Bible speak for itself. Wesley believed that every text should be taken in its literal meaning if it's not contrary to the meaning of other texts. If such contradiction is found, the obscure text must be interpreted by other parallel texts that are clear in their meaning.[9]

Unity and Continuity of Development in the Bible. This leads us into a third guideline for studying the Bible in a Wesleyan spirit. Wesley indicated his acceptance of the essential unity and continuity of the Scriptures even though it was written by 40 inspired writers living in vastly different circumstances. He rightly observed, after prolonged meditation on the Holy Scriptures, that a reason for believing that the Bible must be from God is "the goodness of the doctrine, and the moral character of the penmen."[10]

In the Protestant doctrine of *sola scriptura* (Scripture alone) there is no effort or desire to make an idol of the Bible. The Wesleyan is interested in the Bible's ideas. It is understood that all theological reflection must be aligned with Scripture. When the Bible is studied as a whole, then the unity and continuity of the Bible provides us with the solid content for our practice and rule of faith.

God's Revelation. One other guideline deals with God's revelation for our response. God speaks to us through His Word. In the spirit of Wesley we would say that the Bible must come alive to the reader and the hearer. How does that happen? It is not by accident. It is by returning again and again to the Scriptures, by meditating prayerfully on the Word, by listening to the voice of God, and by sharing in the fellowship of believers who seek to know and love God better.[11] This means we will listen when the Bible is read in church, preached, sung in hymns, and read responsively. All are typical of Wesley's emphasis upon the necessity of Scripture and worship. It is time for the Bible to become a living book to us, as we read and study it diligently to know more of Christ who is revealed in it.

Fundamental, Liberal, Wesleyan Alternatives

Fundamentalists have been just as guilty as liberals in substituting Scripture for the living Christ. The danger is to see only half the truth in assuming one position or the other. Some Fundamentalists emphasize the divine source of the Bible to the extent that they neglect the human origin. Some liberals stress the human and forget (if they do not actually deny) the divine. The Bible has its divine origin, for the Holy Spirit inspired the writers. It also had its human origin, for it came from the hands of men who wrote it.

The Wesleyan alternative insists upon the *internal* witness, both individually and corporately. The Bible proves itself, but, more importantly, the "experience [within believers] of the authenticating voice of the Living Word clinches the matter."[12]

What is reading the Bible in a Wesleyan mode? There are some basic theological points in Wesleyan theology that are critical to Bible reading and study.[13]

Optimism of Grace; Pessimism of Nature. It must be understood that as Wesleyans we are absolute pessimists about human nature apart from the saving grace of God. We have, however, an absolute optimism about what grace can do in us. Grace has no limits! We are not striving to gain salvation but striving to express it. We strive to "have the mind of Christ" (1 Corinthians 2:16) in this life.

Prevenient Grace. As Wesleyans, we believe the Holy Spirit is always and everywhere at work, among all persons and in all persons, seeking to bring them to salvation and sanctification. This means that when a Wesleyan studies the Bible, he or she may be confident that the Holy Spirit will use it. When we teach and preach it, we may be confident of the same work going on. Our Bible study is not so much a matter of digging out some hidden meaning (usually called a "deep thing") as it is a matter of discerning how the Spirit is using His instrument. This means that we study the Bible and hear it preached, expecting that it will (not just *may*) speak to us of how to be Christlike—and this is happening to all.

Free Will. The important point is that we believe that God has granted us grace to say either yes or no to Him. Even after we have said yes at the point of "initial salvation," we are continually called upon to decide in ways and at levels that have to do with salvation itself. This means that in reading and studying the Scriptures, we Wesleyans expect to be *confronted* with significant choices. Scripture not only tells us how we are to use our freedom in such ways as to become like Christ but also is the instrument of the Spirit who confronts us with the necessity of acting on that knowledge.

The doctrine of "once in grace always in grace" approaches the Bible from an entirely different angle. Once among the elect, one studies the Bible to know what to do and how to express what one is in Christ, but one does this on the basis of what the Bible says, looking largely for *information*. The Wesleyan takes it to be the role of the Bible, as the Spirit's living instrument, to speak to one's current situation, to press the necessity of dynamic Christlikeness, and to ask, "Will you be like Him or not?" This means that we study the Bible constantly faced with basic decisions to be made. Our fate is not already determined, but every outcome awaits the intensely personal decisions we must make.

Assurance. What we have said about free will could be very threatening if it were not for the Wesleyan conviction that the Holy Spirit never leaves us in the dark about our basic relationships to God. As believers, we read the Scriptures, knowing that while we shall be confronted with a new point of decision, the Spirit continually assures us of our salvation. Be it ever so revolutionary, new insight from Scripture is going to affirm us if we are already believers intent on saying, "Yes!"

Being a Christian does not depend on Bible knowledge, but a Christian will seek to know the Bible. We do not cast away our confidence if we run across something new or across something that we simply cannot grasp. The assurance always is that we are a child of God—not some sort of lowly employee, a cousin, or a tool. The assurance is that we will be made Christlike—nothing more, nothing less.

Conclusion

Finally, "Do Wesleyans read the Bible differently?" I believe we do. The Bible for us of the Wesleyan persuasion is the Word of God in human words, but its purpose is not fundamentally to show contradiction between us and God.

Its fundamental purpose is to show how we may become godly in this life. The life, work, and resurrection of Christ are vital to us. We are connected to God through our Lord Jesus Christ. Jesus is not an ideal or contradiction to us. Rather, He is Life! The Word of God is a written revelation of Jesus Christ. The law is not set against the gospel. Christ is the Living Word, and the Bible is the written Word.

The role of Scripture is to encourage us to be Christlike without denying the sinfulness of our nature apart from grace. We do not have to be contradictory to Christ. The Word gives us God's perspective on life. We believe we do live in the Kingdom and that we do see things as God sees them.

Background Scripture: Isaiah 55:8; Matthew 15:2-3, 6; Luke 4:32; 24:25-27; 1 Corinthians 2:16; 2 Timothy 3:16

Memory Verses: Matthew 22:37-39

Dr. Jay Hunton is senior pastor of the Church of the Nazarene in Santa Rosa, California.

1. Grant Osborne and Stephen Woodward, *Handbook for Bible Study* (Grand Rapids: Baker Book House, 1979), 11.

2. Thomas Jackson, ed., *The Works of the Rev. John Wesley, A.M. with the Last Corrections of the Author* (London: Wesleyan-Methodist Book Room, 1829-31), 3:267.

3. Colin Williams, *John Wesley's Theology Today* (Nashville: Abingdon Press, 1960), 23-29.

4. Albert Outler, ed., *John Wesley: Letters to James Harvey* (New York: Oxford University Press, 1964), 70-73.

5. Paul Merritt Bassett, "The Holiness Movement and the Protestant Principle," *Wesleyan Theological Journal* 19 (Spring 1983): 12-13.

6. G. J. Cuming, "Collect for the Second Sunday in Advent" in *The Durham Book: The Revision of the Book of Common Prayer* (Westport, Conn.: Greenwood Press, 1961), 102.

7. John Wesley, *Explanatory Notes upon the New Testament* (London: Epworth Press, 1954), 794.

8. Mack B. Stokes, *The Bible in the Wesleyan Heritage* (Nashville: Parthenon Press, 1981), 84.

9. Wesley, *Explanatory Notes*, 570.

10. Bassett, "Protestant Principle," 9.

11. Paul Merritt Bassett, "The Fundamental Leavening of the Holiness Movement, 1914-1940. The Church of the Nazarene: A Case Study," *Wesleyan Theological Journal* 13 (Spring, 1978): 65.

12. Ibid., 75.

13. I am indebted to Dr. Paul Bassett for many of these excerpts, which I gleaned from a lecture he gave in 1987 at Nazarene Theological Seminary.

11

The Bible
Tells Me So

by Wayne McCown

THE CROWD STILLED TO HEAR HIS RESPONSE. The
Chicago reporter had asked boldly, "What is the most important truth you have discovered in your studies?"

Karl Barth was in the spotlight, and the cameras were
rolling. A German theologian, he had become world famous for his many, large scholarly books. But he replied
simply, without hesitation, "Jesus loves me, this I know, for
the Bible tells me so."

His answer made the headlines. It was stunning for
both its brevity and its simplicity. It was indeed a powerful
statement on "truth." At the heart of it was the good news
of God's love for us, as told in the Bible.

Barth was right. That Book, which tells us of God's
love, is special. It is powerful. It is authoritative. Why? Not
simply because the Church says so; rather because the Bible truly is God's Word.

The Bible itself tells us that God's Word is powerful, living, and dynamic (see Hebrews 4:13-14). When He sends it
forth, it does not return "void" but accomplishes its intended purpose (see Isaiah 55:10-11). It is the power of God for
salvation, but it also brings judgment (see Romans 1:16-18).

Orthodox Christians have always held the Bible in
high regard. Contemporary Wesleyans do too. Our pur-

pose in this chapter is to explore the reasons for this regard.

God Has Spoken . . . to Us

Hebrews 1:1-3 declares that the same God who spoke to the prophets of old has spoken to us.

> *In the past God spoke to our forefathers* through the prophets at many times and in various ways, *but in these last days he has spoken to us by his Son,* whom he appointed heir of all things, and through whom he made the universe. The Son is the radiance of God's glory and the exact representation of his being, sustaining all things by his powerful word. After he had provided purification for sins, he sat down at the right hand of the Majesty in heaven *(emphasis added).*

Indeed, God has revealed himself to us—in person, deed, and word.

The authority of the Bible is based, in the first and most important sense, on the fact that it represents *the unique record of God's special revelation to us.* It records the event of God's revelation to us in the person of His Son. "Anyone who has seen me," Jesus declared, "has seen the Father" (John 14:9). Though fully God, He came in human flesh to show us the Father's love (see Philippians 2:5-8). Moreover, the Bible tells us of Jesus' death on a cross for our sins, of His resurrection and victory over death, and of His ascension to the right hand of God.

Indeed, the Bible records how God has throughout history revealed himself in mighty acts. Thus, He brought judgment on Egypt and defeated the enemies of Israel. He preserved His people in the wilderness and delivered them from the jaws of death. The Bible tells us, in story after story, how God acted on behalf of His own, revealing His power and His salvation.

The Bible also records how God has spoken to humanity, through visions, commandments, and prophecies. The

Bible preserves for us God's spoken words, as declared through Moses and the prophets, Jesus and the apostles.

No other book contains such a revelation of God in person, deed, and word.

Moreover, according to the testimony of the Bible itself, *God inspired the written record* of this revelation. The human authors did not simply write as they chose but as the Holy Spirit "moved" them (2 Peter 1:21, KJV).

Second Timothy 3:16 declares, "All scripture is inspired by God" (NRSV). In the Greek text "inspired by God" is a single word, signifying "God-breathed." Such is the claim of Scripture. Many believers have confirmed its claim, sensing God's presence as they read.

Second Timothy 3:16-17 also declares that the Bible is not only inspired but "is useful for teaching, for reproof, for correction, and for training in righteousness, so that everyone who belongs to God may be proficient, equipped for every good work" (NRSV).

The doctrine of inspiration embraces not only the initial authors but contemporary readers as well. God's Spirit is still tending to this Word, helping us understand, interpret, and apply it. And as we do, we grow up in salvation (see 1 Peter 2:2) and are prepared for ministry to others.

The Bible (which we call the Word of God) is *regarded* by the Christian Church as authoritative in matters of faith and practice.

Wesleyans believe that this authority is essential and inherent to the Word itself. At this point, however, the Christian church is making a statement about itself.

As Joshua declared, "Choose for yourself . . . , but as for me and my household, we will serve the Lord" (24:15). In the same way we declare that, since the Bible is God's inspired Word and reveals to us the way of salvation, it will be our normative guide in matters of Christian faith and practice.

When playing certain word games, it helps to agree on

a specific dictionary as a final court of appeal. Otherwise, we must argue over the introduction of made-up words and foreign languages. Similarly in the Christian Church, we agree to subject all opinions on matters of faith to the test of God's Word. It is our commonly recognized authority and normative guide.

God Cannot Lie

Throughout the Scriptures we are assured that God is truthful and trustworthy. His Word partakes of the same qualities, as declared in the following scriptures.

Paul, a servant of God and an apostle of Jesus Christ for the faith of God's elect and the knowledge of the truth that leads to godliness—a faith and knowledge resting on the hope of eternal life, which *God, who does not lie*, promised before the beginning of time, and at his appointed season he brought his word to light through the preaching entrusted to me by the command of God our Savior, to Titus, my true son in our common faith: grace and peace from God the Father and Christ Jesus our Savior *(Titus 1:1-4, emphasis added).*

Men swear by someone greater than themselves, and the oath confirms what is said and puts an end to all argument. Because God wanted to make the unchanging nature of his purpose very clear to the heirs of what was promised, he confirmed it with an oath. God did this so that, by two unchangeable things in which *it is impossible for God to lie*, we who have fled to take hold of the hope offered to us may be greatly encouraged *(Hebrews 6:16-18, emphasis added).*

The Bible's record of God's revelation has been *proved historically accurate.* Archaeological finds, in particular during the past two centuries, have shed new light on Bible backgrounds. In every instance, they have confirmed the accuracy of God's Word.

In the early 19th century, there was considerable doubt in scholarly circles regarding the historical accuracy of Acts.

Sir William Ramsey, a wealthy archaeologist, set out to prove that the biblical account was fictitious. As he pursued the journeys of Paul, however, at site after site Ramsey turned up evidence supporting rather than refuting Luke's account. That story has been repeated many times for other parts of Scripture. Historical evidence, where available, attests to the accuracy of the biblical record.

Further, although written over a period of approximately 1,500 years, the Bible *reflects a coherent unity* of religious belief and experience.

Admittedly, contemporary biblical scholarship emphasizes diversity more than unity. Orthodox Christianity, on the other hand, has always sought out the common themes within the literary collection called the Scriptures. Progressive revelation and the development of ideas are recognized. Differing expressions of faith are acknowledged. But the ultimate goal is to discover the theological truths revealed for our benefit in this record.

That is not an impossible task. The major themes and teachings (doctrines)—such as sin, salvation, law, and grace—are easily identified. Moreover, they show a remarkable coherence in their development and presentation.

The central message—God's promise of salvation through Jesus Christ—is clearly communicated in the Bible. The promises spoken by the patriarchs and prophets of the Old Testament find their fulfillment in the New Testament. One does not have to be a scholar to understand what God has revealed to us concerning our need and the remedy He offers. While there may be some passages that are difficult to interpret, most of the Bible can be readily understood.

It is instructive to note that the form of Greek used by the New Testament writers is that of the common people, not a higher, literary form. This signifies God's attempt to reveal, rather than hide, himself and His Word to us. He communicated the central message—salvation in Jesus Christ—not only in understandable language but in person as well.

God's Word Is Living and Active

The Bible's authority does not reside within the pages of the book. Rather, it represents a living and dynamic presence at work within the lives of God's people.

The word of God is living and active. Sharper than any double-edged sword, it penetrates even to dividing soul and spirit, joints and marrow; it judges the thoughts and attitudes of the heart. Nothing in all creation is hidden from God's sight. Everything is uncovered and laid bare before the eyes of him to whom we must give account *(Hebrews 4:12-13, emphasis added).*

The trustworthiness of the Bible has been affirmed by many persons, as *a reliable resource and guide for life.* While it is possible to misuse the Bible (and its authority), to place oneself under its authority is to find a strong and dependable source of comfort, inspiration, and guidance.

Most books, once read, are set aside, rarely to be used again. But for many believers across the centuries, this Book has become a daily companion from which they have mined treasures of encouragement and wisdom for the living of life. They testify that their lives have been greatly enriched thereby. Such is the nature of the ongoing, dynamic ministry of God's Word in the hearts, minds, and spirits of His people.

Moreover, many believers can attest to the *adequacy* of the Bible to accomplish in our lives what God intends and promises. This is not a Word that disappoints or fails us. (More often than not, we are the ones at fault.) God stands behind His Word, and it is powerful to fulfill His promises to us.

We can put our faith in God; we can trust His Word. He is faithful; His Word is dependable. We have the Bible.

It is a sufficient and complete source of truth; we need nothing more.

Indeed, the *power of God* is at work in us when we study, believe, and obey God's Word. As God's Word lives in us, so His presence lives in us. Thus the Word of God internalized (through hearing, reading, studying, memorizing, and meditating on it) cleanses us and empowers us for service

Hearing (or reading) the Word, however, is not enough. We must also act on it. As James says, "Do not merely listen to the word, and so deceive yourselves. Do what it says" (1:22). Obedience is a necessary companion to faith.

At the close of the Sermon on the Mount, Jesus tells a parable of two builders. On the one hand, says Jesus, the person "who hears these words of mine and does *not* put them into practice" (Matthew 7:26, emphasis added) is like a foolish builder who built his house (i.e., life) on sand. On the other hand, the person "who hears these words of mine and puts them into practice" (v. 24) is like a wise builder who built his house (i.e., life) on a solid foundation.

Jesus' words recorded in the Bible are a solid foundation on which to build one's life. But hearing—even attentive hearing—is not enough. One must also act on them, do them, build on them.

Biblical authority is not merely doctrinal. Rather, it is dynamic, a living presence. It is God's presence at work within us as we act on it, obey its commands, and cling to its promises. The Bible is authoritative because it is God's Word, living and powerful to accomplish God's purposes in and for us.

We must pay more careful attention, therefore, to what we have heard, so that we do not drift away. For if the message spoken by angels [i.e., the Mosaic Law] was binding, and every violation and disobedience received its just punishment, how shall we escape if we ignore such a great salvation? This salvation, which was first announced by the Lord, was confirmed to us by those who heard him. God also testified to it by signs, wonders and various miracles, and gifts of the Holy Spirit distributed according to his will *(Hebrews 2:1-4, emphasis added)*.

Background Scripture: Joshua 24:15; Isaiah 55:10-11; Matthew 7:24; 26; John 14:9; Romans 1:16-18; Philippians 2:5-8; Titus 1:14; Hebrews 1:1-3; 2:1-4; 4:12-14; 6:16-18; James 1:22; 1 Peter 2:2; 2 Peter 1:21; 3:16-17

Memory Verse: 1 Peter 1:23

Dr. Wayne McCown is senior vice president and provost at Roberts Wesleyan College in Rochester, New York.

12

The Bible in Everyday Life

by Gene Van Note

"WANTED: YOUNG, SKINNY, WIRY FELLOWS over 18. Must be expert riders. Willing to risk death daily. Orphans preferred. Wages $25 a week."

In early 1860, this classified ad appeared in the San Francisco and Sacramento newspapers. The Russell, Majors, and Waddell transportation firm was looking for 80 young men to become riders for a new postal service, the Pony Express.

Each Pony Express rider carried a pouch filled with 15 to 20 pounds of mail, costing $5 an ounce. He was also given a Bible. Part of the oath each Pony Express rider took on entering the service was to read and live by the Holy Bible—even in the lawless cities of the Wild West.

We no longer expect our mail carrier to have a Bible in his or her mail sack, but the Bible continues to have a significant place in our history. Nowhere is this more evident than when a public official, including the president of the United States, takes the oath of office with his or her hand on an open Bible.

The Place of the Bible Among English-speaking People

In the early 1600s, an English playwright was known as Wm Shaxpere, Willm Shagspere, William Shackspeare,

Wm Shackespe, Willmus Shakspere, and simply Shaxberd. He is now known only and always as William Shakespeare.

William Tyndale's translation of the New Testament, published in 1526, had 11 different spellings of the word we now spell "if."

What made the difference? The Holy Bible, particularly the King James Version, and the plays of William Shakespeare. The King James Version was printed in 1611, about the time when the Bard of Avon was becoming known. Historians of the English language say that the combined impact of the Bible and the plays of Shakespeare gave the language form and stability, which is good news except for those of us who have a hard time spelling correctly.

The British historian Lord Macaulay said, "The English Bible is a book which if everything else in our language should perish, would alone suffice to show the whole extent of its beauty and power."

The Bible has and continues to be the standard, not only for the English language but for ethical living and political morality. But, for Christians, the Bible has a stabilizing power that goes far beyond what any of these have suggested.

The Centrality of the Bible in Protestantism

The apostle Paul reminded his young colleague, Timothy, of the power of God's Word when he said, "From childhood you have known the sacred writings that are able to instruct you for salvation through faith in Christ Jesus." Then he added, "All scripture is inspired by God and is useful for teaching, for reproof, for correction, and for training in righteousness, so that everyone who belongs to God may be proficient, equipped for every good work" (2 Timothy 3:15-16, NRSV).

The critical importance of the Bible for Christian living was one of the rediscoveries of the Protestant Reformation led by Martin Luther. His careful study of Romans and Galatians led him to see that only the Holy Bible, combined with faith in God and not the traditions of the Church, could bring freedom from sin.

Luther insisted that all religious experience must be tested by the Bible, for it is the final authority. John Wesley agreed. "The Scriptures are the touchstone whereby Christians examine all, real or supposed, revelations," Wesley said in one of his letters.[1]

So great was John Wesley's commitment to the Word of God that, though he published 233 books and encouraged his preachers to read other books in addition to the Bible, he called himself a man of one book. The Bible stood alone as the final authority for belief and practice. In 1728 he wrote, "I want to know one thing—the way to heaven; how to land safe on that happy shore. God himself has condescended to teach the way. . . . He had written it down in a book. O give me that book! At any price give me the book of God! . . . Let me be a man of one book."[2]

In the spirit of Wesley, let us look at some practical ways we can use the Holy Bible to learn about God, our world, our church, and ourselves.

The Bible and Personal Spiritual Growth

A little boy asked his friend, "Why does your grandmother read the Bible so much?"

"She's studying for her finals," came the reply.

We understand that. But, in all honesty, most of us spend more time trying to cope with the demands of living than the implications of dying.

And so we ask, how can the Bible help us face the daily challenges of life?

A place to begin is *devotional Bible study*, built on the conviction that the Bible, as the Word of God, is the final authority on all matters of faith and Christian living, containing everything we need to know for our salvation.

Standing on that foundation, here are some suggestions for using the Bible devotionally:

Begin with prayer. If it's true, as Paul declared to Timothy that "all scripture is inspired by God" (2 Timothy 3:16, NRSV), then it follows that it might help to talk with the Author. There's no better place to begin our Scripture study than with a prayer that we will be given increased understanding of His holy Word.

Read the Bible before reading *about* the Bible. The Bible is not a book of puzzles. Nor is it a collection of mysterious writings. To be sure, we'll need help to grasp some portions of the Bible, but nearly all of the Bible is easily understandable, even by the beginner. Read longer rather than shorter passages; read a full chapter or a book at a time. Read to discover what the writer was trying to say to the first people who read it.

Then, don't hesitate to read about the Bible. We rely on experts in other areas of our lives. We take our cars to mechanics and our bodies to medical doctors. It makes just as much sense to take our questions about the Word to those who have spent a lifetime learning about it. Not every scholar's work is of equal value, so read with discrimination. But read, nevertheless.

Devotional Bible study employs a variety of tools. Read the same scriptural passage from several different translations. Read about the same event, or biblical truth, from different authors. For example, both Matthew and Luke tell us about the birth of Jesus, but their stories are not identical. And these need to be "fleshed out" by reading the prophecies of His birth in the Old Testament.

Meditate. This spiritual discipline can take a wide variety of forms, from sitting in a rocking chair with an apple and your Bible in the early morning to a week spent in silence in a retreat setting. However we do it, we need to let the message of God's Word "soak in" once in awhile. Many people have found some form of meditating on the Word to be a helpful daily discipline.

Memorize. The psalmist wrote, "I have hidden your word in my heart that I might not sin against you" (119:11). Some people memorize a Bible verse and let it guide them through the day while they're doing their work or driving on the freeway. In fact, meditation on the Word that calms the soul might increase our life expectancy on some crowded highways. I can still recall the calmness I experienced when, at a time of great stress, I repeated again and again these words I learned many years earlier, "Thou wilt keep him in perfect peace, whose mind is stayed on thee: because he trusteth in thee" (Isaiah 26:3, KJV).

The Bible and Healthy Relationships

More people would volunteer to become monks if they could have pizza delivered to their monastic cells. We need the interaction with life and with other people that sharing a pizza brings, but bumping into people can cause bruises. Unfortunately, the wounds that take the longest to heal are those that damage the spirit and fracture the relationship between persons. The Bible can help us because the Bible speaks so often and so clearly to our human condition.

Long-range study that comes with careful planning allows the Bible to deal with stressful issues without it taking on the nature of a personal attack. If the teacher says, "We're going to look at what the Bible says about anger because Jones had a nasty attitude in our last board meeting," Jones probably won't change and people will choose sides. But when we're studying God's Word, it's uncanny how the Holy Spirit works out the timing so that our Bible study deals with the issues troubling the larger group. When that happens, no one is on the spot, except as the Holy Spirit focuses the spotlight of the Word. As Paul said, "All scripture is inspired by God and is useful for teaching, for reproof, for correction, and for training in righteousness" (2 Timothy 3:16, NRSV).

Many people seek out a small group of like-minded Christians who will covenant with each other to allow the Bible to lead them toward spiritual maturity. These groups, meeting regularly, provide support and accountability. These vary widely in form, from a group of men at breakfast once a week to persons who agree to meet regularly in a disciplined study of the Word and careful accountability to each other. Then the Bible becomes the guide not only in personal living and spiritual growth but also in the development of healthy relationships with others.

While there are some dangers in small-group Bible study, they can easily be avoided by counseling with the pastor during the preparatory stage of a group.

The Bible and Worship

Actually, worship is not a new theme in this chapter. We've been looking at worship from a personal point of view. Now we turn to the church gathered together at a specified time for the purpose of giving praise and honor to the Lord.

As we've already noted, the Bible has had a central place in Protestant worship. The primacy of the Word in evangelical churches is symbolized by the placement of the pulpit in the middle of the platform. From that central position the Word is read and preached. The grace of God is mediated to us through the written Word.

Few of us are asked to plan a worship service. Thus, we have little input and less control over the form our worship takes. We can, however, nudge our worship leaders toward Bible-centered worship. Prayer and encouragement can help move our worship from a recitation of human accomplishment to greater focus on the Word. Subtle things like bringing our Bible and following as the preacher reads seem small but can have great influence.

Perhaps the most important thing we need to do is to recover the art of *listening* to the Word. We live in a time when most of our information and entertainment is delivered electronically. The TV screen and the computer monitor are our windows to the world. The written Word, and its explanation, seem to come from some ancient civilization. Yet, it is still God's living Word to us. We may need to learn some new skills, but we must recover the art of listening to the ministry of the Word as it is shared with us. Perhaps there is nothing greater we can do as laypersons toward greater use of the Bible in our worship than to increase our listening skills.

And with it all comes the realization that understanding and obedience go hand-in-hand. The truth will set us free only as and when we decide to put it into practice.

Background Scripture: Psalm 119:11; Isaiah 26:3; 2 Timothy 3:15-16

Memory Verse: James 1:22

Rev. Gene Van Note is the former executive editor of adult Sunday School materials for the Church of the Nazarene. He is retired and lives in Overland Park, Kansas.

---

1. John Telford, ed., *The Letters of the Rev. John Wesley, A.M.* (London: Epworth Press, 1931), 117.
2. W. P. Harrison, ed., *The Wesleyan Standards* (Nashville: Publishing House of the M.E. Church, South, 1912), 17.

13

Melting and Molding

by Carl M. Leth

I love to tell the story; 'Tis pleasant to repeat
What seems each time I tell it More wonderfully sweet.

. . . .

I love to tell the story, For those who know it best
Seem hungering and thirsting To hear it like the rest.
("I Love to Tell the Story," Katherine Hankey)

As a young boy I remember watching the lined, leathery face of an old farmer as he sang these words. How could they be true? Surely the story must get old, tiring, and familiar. Yet I watched that grizzled, old saint change as he sang about "the old, old story." There was an almost childlike anticipation at the thought of hearing the old story once more. I was both fascinated and puzzled by what I saw happening. With the passing of time I find that I understand more clearly the old farmer's eagerness for the Word. I am discovering what that old farmer knew. The story just keeps getting better.

There is something enduring and powerful about the "story." The Bible is not a book to be read, analyzed, and put on the shelf to gather dust. God's Word given to us in the Bible tells the wonderful, life-changing story of God's love for us and His plan of redemption. It is a story like no other. These chapters have brought us to a better understanding and deeper appreciation of this treasure. As we come to the end of this study we want to conclude with a sense of beginning. We have only begun what can be a life-long journey with this Word that holds continuing meaning and power for us.

Power to Transform

James describes the power of the Word to change us:

Therefore, get rid of all moral filth and the evil that is so prevalent and humbly accept the word planted in you, which can save you. Do not merely listen to the word, and so deceive yourselves. Do what it says. Anyone who listens to the word but does not do what it says is like a man who looks at his face in a mirror and, after looking at himself, goes away and immediately forgets what he looks like. But the man who looks intently into the perfect law that gives freedom, and continues to do this, not forgetting what he has heard, but doing it—he will be blessed in what he does (1:21-25).

He understands that the Word can work powerfully in us to transform us. He uses the analogy of a mirror to portray it. When we look in an earthly mirror, we see only the reflection of what we are. The physical mirror only shows us as we appear on the outside. God's Word also reveals us. Unlike a common mirror, however, God's Word does more than reflect superficial appearances. It reflects back a truer picture of who we are than any mirror could. It probes deeply into who we are to show us what God sees. The mirror of God's Word not only reveals us but also changes us as we look into it. Its reflection includes a multifaceted image of what we truly are and what we can, by grace, become.

By focusing on Scripture's "reflection," we enter the process of transformation. Through the intentional searching of God's Word we are changed from what we are into what God wants to produce in us. It is generally true that we become increasingly like the values and models on which we focus. Jesus alluded to this in Matthew 6:22-23 when He spoke of the power of the "eye." The focus of the eye determines the character of the life.

Fans of J. R. Tolkien will recognize a negative example of this in the character of Gollum in *The Hobbit* and *Lord of the Rings* trilogy. We meet Gollum early in the story. What a repulsive figure he is! He is a creature of darkness in every sense. Alone, in a deep mountain cavern, he lives only for the dark magic ring he calls his "precious." He stands in stark contrast to the hero who is a creature called a "hobbit." Hobbits are cheerful little creatures who enjoy social life and parties and are simple, bright, and disarmingly childlike. It is only at the very end of the trilogy of the *Rings* that we learn Gollum's true identity. At one time he, too, was a hobbit. A lifetime of treasuring the dark magic ring had transformed him from the bright creature he had been into the twisted, demented creature he had become.

If this were true only in stories, we could ignore or dismiss it. Unfortunately, the reality of this parable-like story is all too true. People are transformed by the focus of their lives, the things they value and intently pursue. Some are darkly transformed by anger or bitterness. Some are bent by pursuit of sexual fulfillment. Some are shaped by desire for success or material possessions. We can be certain that the object of our attention and desire will shape us.

James is saying (in 1:21-25) that the transforming power of the Word is available to us. If we will use it, focus intently upon it, and allow it to shape us, it will transform us. In Romans Paul calls us to this kind of transformation. "Do not conform any longer to the pattern of this world, but be transformed by the renewing of your mind. Then you will be able to test and approve what God's will is—his good, pleasing and perfect will" (12:2). Paul describes a continuing process of inner transformation. That transformation is enabled by the Holy Spirit but is accomplished primarily through the Word.

This means that Scripture is a special form of "literature." It is not so much about knowledge as it is about spiritual and character formation. It is not primarily addressed to the head but to the heart and life. It is not given to inform us but to transform us. We are invited to gaze intently into the Word until "we, who with unveiled faces all reflect the Lord's glory, are being transformed into his likeness with ever-increasing glory" (2 Corinthians 3:18).

Melting and Molding

We might compare how Scripture works to the work of a foundry and mill. The process usually begins with raw materials. Rough and unpromising, they are valuable only in their potential. Unless the useful elements can be drawn out, they will remain unproductive. Often, scrap materials are also used. Used up, broken, or cast off, they, too, have little value as they are. Some are even the discarded results of earlier failures. In appearance they are not very promising resources. All are cast together into the melting and molding process.

In the foundry it is heat that begins the refining process. Intense, uncomfortable, melting heat. Former shapes gradually wilt. At first it must seem to be destructive, but the purpose of the process is soon clear. The waste materials are revealed, rising to the top. Elements that hinder the discovery of the valuable metal are drawn off. What remains is refined, ready to be useful.

The value of the refined metal is still in its potential. The melting is accompanied by the process of molding. The metal is shaped. It is poured, extruded, stamped, and rolled. Its potential is realized by skillful molding into useful and productive materials. The process completes its cycle by transforming the seemingly useless into something valuable.

Scripture works like that in our lives. Through it, the Holy Spirit works like a refining fire, revealing and removing things that are unworthy and unholy. At the same time the Holy Spirit works through Scripture to shape us. It takes unproductive potential and makes it fruitful and productive. Paul uses a play on words (in Greek) to declare this transformation. Speaking of Onesimus (whose name means "useful") Paul says that once he was useless, but now he is useful (Philemon 11). That is the result of the process of God's transforming work in us through the Word. As we allow God to work through His Word to melt and mold us, we will also be able to say, "Once I was useless, but now I am Onesimus [useful]."

Partners in the Process

An important part of "looking" into the Word is our active response to it. James says that we should not only hear the Word but also "do" it. We are called to be active partners in the process of transformation under the authority and guidance of Scripture. Reading the Bible carelessly or indifferently will not be effective in helping us become the people God desires us to be. How can we be effective partners in this wonderfully creative process of personal transformation?

We begin by coming to Scripture in a *teachable spirit.* Our partnership begins with attitude. We don't read the Bible to master it but to allow it to master us. We submit to its judgment. We come as learners willing to be taught. This requires spiritual preparation for the effective study of God's Word. Humility is a necessary attitude and spirit to bring to biblical study. Often we desire to have our lives filled by God. But many times God cannot fill our lives because they are already full. We come to our study of the Bible filled with *our* ideas, agenda, and judgments.

However, humility "empties" us and allows God the opportunity to fill us. We also need to make ourselves vulnerable to God's correction and revelation of our needs and shortcomings. This is always difficult and a little frightening. But we know that God only works through His Word for our good. Even painful lessons are sometimes necessary for our growth. He will not show us what we do not need or cannot bear. We can trust Him.

We continue the process by *intentional discipline.* That is, we apply the lessons of Scripture to our lives on purpose, not by accident. As we bring different attitudes, actions, habits, and values of our lives under the light of Scripture, we are led to make changes. We are prompted to relearn habits and reshape attitudes. We practice making decisions on the basis of biblical principles and values. We check our goals against the test of Scripture. The Bible becomes our daily operating guide for living.

Sometimes we ask God for special, divine guidance unnecessarily. We ask for personal answers when the answers are already clear in the Word. We presume on God when we ignore what He has already said and ask for another (potentially different?) answer. Study of the Word will provide us with God's priorities and values for most situations in life. We need to actively develop a familiarity with them and to apply them to the practical issues and decisions of our lives.

We commit to a *lifelong journey.* Long-term goals and long-term commitments are not a popular part of our culture. We much prefer the instant makeover. Go to the mall and be transformed into a vision of beauty in one hour or less. Go to a weekend retreat or workshop and transform marriage, personality, or finances. But God's plan for us is long-term. God's idea of transformation is not superficial or temporary. He wants to transform our lives through and through. In fact, the process will never be complete in this life. The melting and molding of Scripture is a journey that will fill a lifetime. Let's covenant with God to persistently make that journey.

The Bible as Mystery

We need to add a note about the special character of the Bible. As wonderfully practical as it is, God's Word is much more than practical guidance. It is a holy, God-produced book. While it is useful as a daily guidebook for living, it is also a book of mystery.

I used to have a book about the Bible in my library titled *That Manuscript from Outer Space*. I'm not really comfortable portraying the Bible in extraterrestrial terms, but I do appreciate the sentiment. The Bible is different from any other book. It contains fine literature, interesting history, and lovely poetry. It is, however, more than any of these. It goes "beyond."

I am always intrigued by people who are uncomfortable with God when He chooses to act in ways that don't make sense to us. They conclude that if the message of the Bible appears to contradict human reason, then it must not be true. But the Bible is about a transcendent God. His logic, perspective, and purposes are not reducible to human rationality. Personally, I *want* God to be beyond my rationality. I want Him to be bigger than I am.

In the same way, Scripture is beyond me. I can read it. It is understandable to me. I can learn from it. I know that it is true. But it is still more. It leads me past my limits into the mystery that God is. God's mystery will be more than I can understand. Life lived looking intently into Scripture is life being drawn into the mystery of God.

The Mirror's Deepest Reflection

Despite the Bible's element of mystery, we can know the image that it will reflect most deeply. We can even attach a face to the vision that God wants to reproduce in us. John expressed that truth when he wrote, "Dear friends, now we are children of God, and what we will be has not yet been made known. But we know that when he appears, we shall be like him" (1 John 3:2). The reflection of the mirror that transforms me, the image like which I am becoming, is the likeness of Jesus Christ.

The discovery of the melting and molding of Scripture is the discovery of Christ's likeness in us. The search for the deepest reflection of the mirror of God's Word is expressed in the words of this chorus:

Let the beauty of Jesus be seen in me—
All His wonderful passion and purity!
O Thou Spirit divine, All my nature refine
Till the beauty of Jesus be seen in me.
("Let the Beauty of Jesus Be Seen in Me,"
Albert Orsborn)

Endings and Beginnings

We have arrived at the end of our study of the Bible. Hopefully it has been productive, informative, and interesting. More importantly, we hope that this study will serve as a new beginning and not an ending. Whether you are a new Bible reader or a veteran, we invite you to new levels of discovery and transformation as you gaze intently into the Word and allow it to work in your life. What an exciting journey! What a wonderful opportunity! It's time to begin!

Background Scripture: Matthew 6:22-23; Romans 12:2; 2 Corinthians 3:18; Philemon 11; James 1:21-25; 1 John 3:2

Memory Verse: Romans 12:2

Dr. Carl Leth is senior pastor of First Church of the Nazarene in Detroit, Michigan.